ROCKET MAN

THE ROGER CLEMENS STORY

ROCKET MAN

THE ROGER CLEMENS STORY

**Roger Clemens
with Peter Gammons**

THE STEPHEN GREENE PRESS
LEXINGTON, MASSACHUSETTS

First published in 1987 by The Stephen Greene Press, Inc.
Published simultaneously in Canada by Penguin Books
Canada Limited
Distributed by Viking Penguin Inc., 40 West 23rd Street,
New York, NY 10010.

Library of Congress Cataloging-in-Publication Data
Clemens, Roger.
    Rocket man.

    1. Clemens, Roger.   2. Baseball players—United
States—Biography.   3. Boston Red Sox (Baseball team)
I. Gammons, Peter.   II. Title.
GV865.C44A3 1987   796.357′092′4 [B]   86–32025
ISBN 0–8289–0629–7

Book design by Joyce C. Weston
Printed in the United States of America
by Haddon Craftsmen
Set in Trump Mediaeval by AccuComp Typographers
Produced by Unicorn Production Services, Inc.

TO MY MOTHER

CONTENTS

ROCKET MAN

THE ROGER CLEMENS STORY

·1·
AN END AND A BEGINNING

*"Roger has worked hard for everything he's
achieved, and what he's achieved at the age of
twenty-four is beyond any of our family's
imaginations. What some people may not understand
about him is that he is from a strong, close
family background, and as far as he's concerned,
the most important thing he'll remember in 1986
is the birth of Koby Aaron Clemens."*
— *Randy Clemens,*
Roger's brother

HAVING A BABY was the perfect way to bring an end to a storybook season that went beyond my wildest dreams. It finally put the memory of the World Series and the sixth game to the back of our thoughts, something even the MVP and Cy Young awards hadn't done.

Debbie and I got up on that morning of December 4, finally knowing that the day had come when we'd be parents. I wasn't actually worried that the baby had been due one week earlier on Thanksgiving, as I realized that first babies are often a week or two late. But two days before Thanksgiving the doctor had told us "any day now," and after nine months Deb was ready, so as day after day went by, it seemed like an eternity to her. It seems as if half the time Bruce Hurst and I spent standing in the outfield during batting practice in August and September was spent discussing what I should expect, and he was 100 percent correct about one thing: the last week would be murder.

When we got to Houston Memorial City Hospital that morning, we still didn't know if it would be a boy or a girl. The doctor had said if it were a girl and Deb wanted to get it over quickly that we should put a $50 bill on the table and she'd come grab it in

1

five minutes; I suggested an American Express card. We went in with me pushing her from the back with my camera strap over one shoulder, a diaper bag and another thing of clothes over the other, and the camera in my other hand. I went and got the video camera ready in the delivery room, figuring this would all be rather simple. She had a short labor of six hours, but even though we were unclassified at the hospital, it turned into a circus. Not long before the baby was to come, two nurses popped in and said that every five or ten minutes people were showing up trying to find out if I were here, that they were getting fifteen calls a minute, and that there were flowers. The flowers were nice, but if we were unclassified and supposedly weren't there, how could we accept them? I had to leave, go down to the lobby and get things straightened out, and while I was down there, in came the cameras and crews from all three television stations in Houston as well as a wire service photographer. By that time, they had two policemen guarding our area of the hospital, keeping out everyone but family—of which we had ten or fifteen members.

Finally, I got back to Deb, started the camera rolling, threw on all my doctor clothes, and twenty minutes later—like a miracle— the kid was there. Debbie was amazing. She never screamed at me or anything, and I laughed afterward when I called Jim Rice at home and he said, "All it would take for most of us is to go through this once and we'd never do it again." While all this was going on, Deb could have asked me for anything and I'd have given it to her. I was so excited that I couldn't remember everything, which is why it's so important that we have it all on tape. When he—actually still "it" at that point, since we didn't know yet if it was a boy or a girl—came down you can hear me saying "look at this hair." It's a good thing my sister had warned me about the oblong head and the wrinkled ears and the purple color, for even then when he came out I was playing twenty questions, starting with "what's wrong with his ear?" I kept telling everyone "be careful, be careful," telling a doctor who had delivered about a million babies what to do and making him sweat bullets.

"It looks like you've got yourself a boy," the doctor announced, and the ten or fifteen people in the hallway woke up every mother in the wing. My mother was down on her knees pounding on the floor, my sister was crying, my in-laws were cheering, and it sounded like someone had hit a home run. Not that I was really any better. My eyes were filled with tears, and I could barely take the four or five Polaroid shots, three of which I took to the hallway so people could see him. Koby Aaron. That had already been decided, if he was a boy. It was going to be either Kris or Koby, although if we'd won the World Series, we might have had Shea for a middle name.

When Koby came out and I saw that everything was normal and he had his hands and fingers and feet, I had the most unbelievable sensation I've ever experienced. Hurst and other teammates had told me that it would be the greatest feeling of my life, but until it happened, I didn't know what they meant. We were so in awe we didn't realize that he screamed as much as he did, and in one of his first breaths he overextended his right lung, got some fluid in it and had to go under a bubble for a while, which meant we could only hold him for about seven minutes when we wanted half an hour. We didn't realize then what we learned in the first month at home, namely what a temper he has. Deb says he got fighting mad watching me get ejected in Chicago and it affected his personality. I guess we won't know for years how the World Series affected him.

I do know that the World Series affected me, at least until Koby was born. In fact, the whole postseason had an effect on me so that it sort of runs together, in a way that makes it difficult sometimes to focus on any one aspect or game. I don't know that I ever quite got in sync, there were so many distractions and so much was going on.

I guess it isn't completely surprising that despite all the good things that happened in the play-offs and Series, what fans seem to remember most is the sixth game of the Series. But I don't think about the two-strike Mets hits or the wild pitch or the final ground ball as much as I do the blister that forced me out after the seventh inning. Somehow, that silly blister was one of those things that kept me asking "why *then*?" for weeks. I thought so little about the blister at the time that immediately after that game I couldn't even really remember when it happened. All I recalled was that the pitch was a slider, and I was frustrated with that pitch. I gave up four hits—three on sliders. It got like Strat-O-Matic automatic— throw a slider to a left-hander and he pulls it through the hole. That's what I was thinking about in the fifth inning of the sixth game of the Series. That and that I felt extremely confident. This was our year, my year, and I was where I had always wanted to be: on the mound in the game that could clinch it. And for the first time since I got hit in the elbow in my last regular season start, October 1, I felt the way I had all season.

It was later that I remembered the pitch. It was the fifth inning, which I'd started with a 2–0 lead and a no-hitter, walked Darryl Strawberry, had him steal second and score on a backup slider Ray Knight hit up the middle. The pitch was a slider to Mookie Wilson. What I remember most is that I didn't throw it where I wanted to. I meant to get the ball in on his fists, but I left it too far over the plate, he pulled it through the hole and got Knight over to third, which enabled him to score the tying run on a double play ball. The blister tore as I released the slider, and it started bleeding— so badly that before I finished that inning, the umpire threw a couple of balls out of play because of the blood. When I got back to the dugout, Charlie Moss, our trainer, came over and asked to look at it. John McNamara was standing there, too. They started asking me about it, and I told them it was fine, that it didn't hurt my fastball, forkball, or even my curveball. I asked Rich Gedman, my catcher, because he can tell about my stuff better than I can, and he said I was fine. I had thrown a lot of pitches the first time around the order and wasn't overpowering the Mets in the middle innings, but I was pitching, which I think I can do. I figured I could get us to the ninth and let Calvin Schiraldi finish it.

As it turned out, that stupid blister kept it from being a perfect season, at least until Koby was born. When Deb and I got to Winter Haven the first week of February, neither of us ever fantasized about going 24–4, striking out twenty in a game, leading the league in earned run average, starting and winning the All-Star Game in my hometown, winning the division and American League pennant, being voted both the Cy Young and Most Valuable Player awards, and getting some of the other honors that came along. But when things got rolling and Bruce Hurst won the fifth game in Boston to give us the 3–2 lead and I was going into Shea Stadium with a full five days' rest and had 2–0 and 3–2 leads, well, that World Championship ring became the most important goal of all, a goal I had within my grasp.

Until that sixth game, for the entire play-offs and World Series, I had felt as if I were always trying to catch up. And I don't like to operate that way. I always like to keep things in order. When you're a starting pitcher, you live in five day cycles, and when things are going well the way they were this year, it's great that it's happening, but I have to keep it in perspective and not let success get in the way. Two of the five days, I'll talk to the media and talk as much as they want, but I have to get my work in in those other three days. I have my work schedules all planned out before I get to the park, and when it comes to actually pitching, I like to eliminate as many variables as possible and allow instinct to take over. Somehow, I got messed up and behind before the play-off opener against California and never caught up until the sixth game of the Series, four starts later. In that time, I learned as much as I would have from three hundred regular season starts.

Right before the play-offs, someone told me that Dallas Green of the Cubs complained that baseball is the only sport where teams don't go off by themselves. In football, basketball, and hockey, when teams go on the road in the play-offs, they go as a team, but Green said that in baseball, the play-offs and World Series become social events where all the families come along. I know what he meant. We had all sorts of family come in for the play-offs, and I figured that it had gone so smoothly at the All-Star Game, it would be all right here. I was wrong. It was the only time that I ran out of gas, physically and mentally. Right up to a couple of hours before I was supposed to pitch, I was running around trying to get everyone else happy and situated and it seemed like a crisis. Debbie was more than seven months pregnant. I was worrying and I was wearing her out with my exasperation. When I went home for the All-Star Game, I set everyone up and it was easy. Of course, what I forgot was that they knew where the Dome is, where the seats are, and they know where all the things are that they have to do. In Boston, I had to take everyone to his hotel, so I played taxi for two days straight. No one knew where Fenway was; my brother Randy did, but he doesn't know how to get there, he just knew it looks like a warehouse.

When I got to the park and tried to get my proper mental frame of mind, I was ready to relax and collapse. When I went out there, I wasn't prepared. I was just throwing the ball. It wasn't a case of being nervous or anything. I wasn't actually tired—just blah. About eight o'clock, ten minutes before I was supposed to go to the bull pen to begin warming up, I tried to pump myself up. By the second or third inning, I was so pumped up that it was to the point where I couldn't concentrate. California is a dangerous hitting club that kills mistakes, and I was just throwing the ball as hard as I could. Reggie Jackson said later that I was wild in the strike zone, and that was exactly it. Instead of throwing the ball out and away from Brian Downing, I left it over the middle of the plate where he could pull it. And every time they scored another run, I could hear the crowd going *ouch*. That jacked me up even more and got me in bigger trouble. Six runs. An 8–1 loss.

That Saturday night game in Anaheim—the fourth game of the play-offs, when I took the 3–0 lead into the ninth and we ended up losing because I tried to get it over too quickly—I pitched on sheer adrenaline. On the way out I had started to get an infection from all the smoke on the plane, and my system began to break down. It was the same thing flying *back* from California after we had won the unforgettable fifth game. Everyone around me was like a smokestack, and it wiped me out. I was so sick when I pitched the seventh game of the play-offs that not only did Calvin have to come in in the eighth and finish for me, but afterward I couldn't stand up to do all the interviews. I ended up having to do them in a chair. I went back out for the second game of the Series on three days' rest for the third consecutive start, thinking I could do it on adrenaline again, but as Dr. (Arthur) Pappas told me, no matter how strong my arm might be, eventually my body was going to catch up with me and I was going to learn that I'm not as strong as I thought. Although my arm was strong. People kept asking me about my shoulder. Well, right before the end of the season, I went out to Worcester to the University of Massachusetts Medical Center and took Dr. Pappas's battery of tests, and they showed that not only was my shoulder stronger than it had been at the beginning of the season, but it was far stronger than it was when I came out of the University of Texas or went to spring training my rookie season in 1984. So I wasn't physically tired. That infection had worn down my body, I had a 101-degree temperature, and I let my inexperience show when I allowed exterior things like the mound at Shea Stadium get to me. Between starts, I decided that one way to get it out of me was to do something I normally wouldn't—get some things off my chest. Anyway, it was the World Series and I didn't care what people thought; I just wanted to win. I talked to Tom Seaver, and he said that the mound was built up a lot higher than when he was there. My first start there, not only because of the flu, I struggled for four innings before I got any kind of rhythm. As Tom says, pitching's so simple, yet it's so complicated. I came to find out that I can make a two- or three-inch alteration with my legs and that's it, and I was making alterations a lot greater than three inches on a lot of pitches. I found myself not using my legs, so the ball was running up and away and I stopped pushing off to get the ball down. By the fifth inning, McNamara had seen enough. Fortunately, Dwight Gooden didn't have his great stuff or control, Steve Crawford and Bob Stanley pitched really well, and we won, 9–4; and it probably was the best thing to get me out of there, even if I didn't think so at the time. I should have known I was in trouble when I felt better at the plate than I did on the mound.

By getting all the business about the mound off my chest, I figured people would think that I was thinking too much, when really I was just trying to make mental adjustments so I wasn't as flustered. I was starting to get my strength back with all the vitamin B-12 Dr. Pappas was feeding me, and honestly, New York never bothered me. Deb and I had a lot of fun before the Series started, even though I was sick. When I got to my locker before the seventh game of the play-offs, there was a note telling me: "Win or lose, get to New York Thursday for the commercial. For that kind of money, you can smile." I knew it was from my agent, Alan Hendricks. So we went down the next morning, a day earlier than the rest of my teammates, to make the Zest commercial. It was fun because it was something I'd never done before. I had no idea what a major commercial was like. I was lucky, too, because Al Nipper, Mike Greenwell, Jeff Sellers, and I had a bet in September that if we won the division we'd all shave and spike our hair like Bosworth at Oklahoma. I spiked my hair a little for a couple of days, but if I'd gotten that haircut, the commercial people would have told me to take a hike. The bet never really was met; Nipper didn't get much cut, Greenwell didn't have much to cut, and Bedrock Sellers, well it was probably an improvement for him—he's so brain dead he wears his hair like that naturally. I was also hoarse, so I thought I'd better talk like "*Chevvy truucks . . .*," Dick Butkus–style. I had a few lines like, "You're not fully clean unless you're Zestfully clean." They had a guy from Australia who was one of the cameramen from *Legal Eagles*. "Hey mate, I never watched baseball before, mate, but I watched the seventh game of the play-offs just to see what you looked like." On "Good Morning America," they were talking about the marketability of athletes, and they had a clip and said that it took me 242 takes; but that wasn't true. I had five different scenes, and the most takes I had to do was for the last, about 22 or 25. I kept asking them if they were actually going to use my voice. I sound as if I'm going through puberty. My voice was high and sore from yelling and screaming, tired because I didn't get too much sleep. So I talked like *"Chevvy truucks,"* and when we were done we went back to the hotel and went to bed. That commercial made New York fun.

When I went out there for the sixth game, I conditioned myself to the Shea mound the way I have to in Baltimore. It's such a slope that you can't use your legs, built for a junkball pitcher. I was thinking how Gooden kicks back up across the rubber and high, almost turns his letters to the batter. Now I know how he gets his equilibrium. You get that balance point or you're never going to get into position to throw, so I prepared myself. I could tell there was a big difference in my arm from the time I started warming up in the bull pen. In the bull pen before Game Two I didn't have anything, so I figured it would kick in when I got to the mound, as it usually does. It never happened. My arm was still torn down. But in Game Six I had good stuff early. I struck out Lenny Dykstra to start it. I struck out Wally Backman. I struck out six of the nine hitters the first time around the order. I really felt strong early, but then it tailed off a little by the fourth inning. For one thing, the Mets are a good fastball-hitting team, and they don't chase many pitches that run up and out of the strike zone. The other thing was that Gary Carter, Strawberry, and Rafael Santana fouled off a ton of pitches their first times up. I think Strawberry fouled off ten. I didn't have the cross-seam fastball that runs and usually gets my strike-outs, and it frustrated me with Carter, Strawberry, and Santana because I couldn't get the ball in on them the way I wanted to.

I lost the no-hitter and the lead in the fifth, but in the sixth—after Backman slapped a fastball for an infield hit and Keith Hernandez hit a slider into center to put runners on first and third, one out—I did what I had to do. I struck out Carter, Strawberry grounded out, and we got a run in the top of the seventh to make it 3–2; and I felt certain we were going to win. One thing Hurst and I talk about is my belief that there are three critical times in a game. The first is the first inning, when a pitcher has to establish himself and set the tempo for the game; I was able to do that in Game Six. The second time is the fourth inning, the second time around the order, when they've seen what you have and you have to start to adjust. The third is any time your team scores. A pitcher *has* to go right out there and shut down the opposition after his team-mates score. That's a big part of winning pitching.

After we got the run in the top of the seventh, I went out and had an easy inning. Fly ball, ground ball, fly ball. But one thing that happened in that inning was that in throwing one last slider—I think it was to Wilson again, why did everything happen with him at the plate that night?—I tore the fingernail off my middle finger and that started bleeding. When I got in from the mound at the end of the inning, the nail was bleeding more than the blister, and when Fischer saw all the blood, he got pretty upset. Mac came over.

"Does it sting?" he asked. I guess he could see that it was shaking.

"Sure, it stings," I told him. "I'm all right, though. I can get you through the eighth, at least. The only thing I can't do is throw a slider, but I can get another inning with my fastball, change of speeds, and my forkball." I was the third hitter that inning, and Fischer told me to go get ready to hit, and that if the first two guys got on, then they'd have to make a decision. Having failed to get down a bunt my first three times up, I figured they didn't have great confidence in me as a hitter.

Dave Henderson led off with a single and Spike Owen bunted him up, and they sent Greenwell up to pinch-hit for me even though we had the lead. What upset me later was that it was made to sound as if I'd asked out of the game. George Grande from ESPN told me about an hour after the game that McNamara had said that I told him that I couldn't go any further. I tried to go see Mac, but Fischer intercepted me and told me that that wasn't what he said. Or meant. I talked to Mac and he said it wasn't what he meant. The fact is that I wanted to keep going. I'd thrown 138 pitches, but I felt as if I'd come through the middle innings and, at worst, could get us to the point where Calvin only needed to get three outs, not six. I think he's better off as a three-out closer. My concentration was outstanding, unlike Game Two. I never heard the crowd; they tell me they were chanting "RO-ger, RO-ger" the way they yelled at Strawberry in Fenway, but I never heard them. About five people have asked me about some woman in the first row behind the screen who had on red gloves and white everything else and was rolling her hands and making funny signs and doing voodoo stuff to distract us; I never saw her, but I want to put the film in the VCR sometime and watch. I didn't see anything. I guess if Greenwell had gotten a hit and scored Henderson and we'd won, nothing would have been said. But I think they were worried too much about the blood. It wasn't worrying me.

I stayed in the dugout and watched to see if Greenwell got a hit, and when he struck out I headed up into the clubhouse to ice my arm. A couple of teammates asked me what I was doing, but I had two thoughts in mind: I wanted to treat my arm properly to begin an off-season I knew had to be in preparation for 1987, and secondly, I had it in the back of my mind that there was always the chance that we'd lose, there'd be a rainout, and I could relieve in a seventh game. I didn't really think we'd lose, even after the Mets tied it at 3–3 in the eighth. The way everything had gone for us and for me personally all year, I never thought about defeat. Even in the fifth game of the play-offs, when we were losing by three runs in the ninth inning and were two outs from being eliminated, I told Hurst that I didn't feel as if it were time for the season to end. And it didn't.

When I'd finished with the ice, I got my jacket and went to the bull pen and watched some of the game. I had to go back inside after Hendu (Henderson) hit the homer leading off the tenth. When we got the two-run lead, the NBC people came into the clubhouse and were setting up the platform. One of the guys said to get the World Championship trophy. I screamed at one of them to keep out and don't bring it in this room until the final out is made. I went back to the bull pen, which is lucky, because I'm glad I didn't see Peter Ueberroth, Mrs. Yawkey, and Haywood Sullivan with Bob Costas, standing there with the World Series trophy and Hurst's MVP trophy with one out to go in the bottom of the tenth.

I've known Calvin for more than five years, and I can watch him walk to the mound and tell what he's going to do by his face. Cal wanted to beat the Mets so badly it was killing him; I guess I'd be the same way if the Red Sox traded me and I came back to face them in the Series. He wanted to stick it to them so badly that when he got the two-run lead and two outs in the tenth, he did exactly what I did in California when we blew the 3–0 lead in the ninth. In Anaheim, I got a quick out, then got two quick strikes on both Dick Schofield and Bob Boone. I hung a slider to Schofield, then got a ball out over the plate to Bob Boone, and Calvin came in—which is when he said he got the brain cramp and threw the curveball that hit Downing and tied it up. I got carried away with the shutout, tried to get them out too quickly and threw pitches that were simply too good. The batters have to be up there hacking in that situation, so you don't want to throw anything too good to hit. I felt like it was me all over again watching Cal in that tenth. He retired the two tough lefties, Backman and Hernandez, had two strikes on Carter. . . .

And made too good a pitch. He gave up the single to Kevin Mitchell, had two strikes on Knight, and gave up another hit; in came Stanley and the two strange plays scored the tying and winning runs. I sat there in front of my locker for a few minutes, head down, extremely upset. Then I realized that I was feeling what the Angels had to have felt. I also realized that we had another game, and my nature is a mixture of confidence and positive thinking. I still thought this was going to be our year, and when we got the rainout the next night and Bruce was going to pitch, I was all fired up again.

Bruce came in after he got the nod to start the first game of the World Series, and he said, "As much as I admire and respect you, it just went up 110 percent. I don't know how you did it all season long. I can't believe it. It's nonstop." Two guys got into a fistfight because they each wanted individual interviews and Bruce wanted them to do it together. By that point, Bruce Hurst was probably the best pitcher in the American League. In September and October, he was almost unbeatable; he'd lost only once in that time, and that was in a meaningless start after we'd clinched the division. That, in itself, was great to be around having been around him for three years. I guess it has something to do with his being rushed up to the big leagues before he was ready and having his confidence shredded, but he'd come to the park almost every day and tell himself that he stunk. When I got hit around my rookie year and was down, he gave me a talk. For two years after that, it seemed as if I were always giving him the same talk. One time I refused to talk to him for three days after he kept saying that he'd be gone in '87, that the Red Sox wanted to get rid of him. That might have been true in the past—I guess they really did offer him to Toronto for

Luis Leal in June 1985—but not after he came up with the split-finger in the second half of that season. In spring training, I tried to tell him that with Bobby Ojeda traded that since he was the oldest starter, he was the leader. He kept telling me I was the leader. But he got off to the good start, and more and more he'd talk with confidence. Then, when he came back from the groin injury, when he was putting it together in late August, he started saying things like, "I *know* I'm good." What a change.

Also, what a difference it meant to me. There were times during the season when I couldn't believe what I heard. When we were on the West Coast trip in July and the only three (of fourteen) games we won were my starts, one night I was sitting in the dugout doing the pitching charts and we were getting blown out early, and I heard both Marty Barrett and Wade Boggs say, "That's all right, we've got Rocket tomorrow." I'm not that good; no one is. But when Bruce got going, I felt as if I could take a deep breath, and the fact that I won eight starts in a row down the stretch says a lot for the pressure he took off me at a time when a lot of teams took runs at us.

We hadn't lost a game that meant anything that Hurst started since August, and to make it even better, when I went out to play some catch and see how my arm was, I felt like I had at the All-Star Game. I thought that I might be able to face two batters, but when I started throwing I felt as if I had at least two innings in me—two innings of good gas, as I did in Houston—and from the time the game started, I was doing a little managing, trying to figure when I'd get in there. Bruce did a great job shutting them out with the 3–0 lead for five innings, but he admitted to me afterward that he simply lost it in the sixth when they scored the three runs and tied it up. He would have finished the sixth with no worse than a 3–1 lead, but told me he got "a little carried away" trying to throw a fastball past Hernandez, one of the best hitters anywhere. Hernandez singled in two runs, and they eventually tied it up.

I was in the bull pen, hoping that I could relieve in the seventh and the eighth. But McNamara had told me before the game, "If it's tied or we're ahead going into the ninth, it's your game." It never got to be my game, obviously, and after that everything in New York became pretty bad. People later misunderstood me when I said that I'd take a fine rather than go back to Shea Stadium for the exhibition game we have with the Mets there in the 1987 season. I have nothing against the fans, who except for a few nuts were fine. It was the security—the police and the way the place was handled. The security guards were screaming at our wives. Calvin's father almost had to take on a half-dozen of them. One guard got up in Deb's face and screamed, "Your husband ——— and we're going to kick his behind." Since she was pregnant, there was no way that in her condition I'd allow her to stay there, so I sent her home to Boston after the sixth game. That might be the one time I'll ever be in a World Series, and I couldn't let my family see the seventh game. There was the fan who threw the golf ball out of the upper deck that just missed Rice's head. When we were coming in from the bull pen after we'd lost the final game, there were all sorts of security guards screaming obscenities at us and calling us all kinds of names. Finally, when we were going across the field to the bus long after it was over and that nut threw the can that hit Jack Rogers, our traveling secretary, in the head, that was it. Jack was lying there on the ground, unconscious, blood spurting from his head, and two New York City cops—with badges and guns—stood there laughing at him. *Laughing.* I started yelling at them and made a move toward one of them. One of them said, "Calm down, son," and I screamed, "My father's been dead since I was nine, I am no kin to you. They ought to blow this place up. Baseball as it oughta be, my foot." They kept replaying Buckner's errors on the message board; then they showed our bench up there as Strawberry was in his home run trot. It got Rice all riled up. The Can got all upset. It was very ugly, something right out of *Rollerball.*

When we got home to Boston, we had no idea what to expect or how the fans felt. It was obvious that everyone was depressed on Tuesday, and most of us went in, cleared out our lockers, went home, and went to sleep. We were being honored on Wednesday by the City of Boston with a parade, and while I had friends who told me a lot of people would show up, I figured it would be a few loyal fans who had it in their hearts to forgive us. There were about twelve or fifteen players, plus McNamara, Fischer, Joe Morgan, and Rene Lachemann, and they put us on a truck and started driving us for Copley Square. The first few blocks seemed like two or three miles—we saw one or two people—and I was thinking this is going to be brutal. Then when we turned the corner onto Boylston Street, I couldn't believe it. The people were ten, twelve, and fifteen deep along the street, and when we got to Government Center it looked

like Woodstock. I had a chill running down my back unlike anything I'd ever experienced. Originally only McNamara and I were
supposed to speak, but when I looked out at half a million people,
then looked around at my teammates, I could see the same excitement in their eyes. Jimmy Rice was so touched, he asked to speak.
So did Barrett. Then Hurst. Even Buckner. Everyone likes to be
loved, but when you come back from losing two games in New
York and you feel devastated because you're thinking that you blew
it and fans show you that kind of emotion, it goes right through
you. We all complain about the fans sometimes. We laugh about
getting booed. But all of us now realize what it is to play in a city
where the fans *care.* Sure, they turned out in Houston after the
Astros were in first place, and I thought I'd been involved in some
sports tradition at the University of Texas, but Boston is a world
unto itself. That parade was the best thing ever.

Two days later, October 31, I was home in Katy, looking back on
the season. A year ago at that time, I was working on weights,
running, and wondering if I'd be able to fully recover from my shoulder operation. Red Sox Public Relations Director Dick Bresciani
and Alan Hendricks had told me that the Cy Young Award would
be announced November 12. They told me to be home at 10:15
in the morning and that Jack Lang, who compiles the votes for
the Baseball Writers Association, would probably call me. I got a
little edgy waiting, because the call came at 10:40, but he managed
to surprise me when he told me that I'd won unanimously. Having
won that first and having heard so much of that mumbo jumbo
that pitchers shouldn't be eligible for the MVP, I figured that when
that was announced six days later that I didn't have much of a
chance. Our baby was due in eight days, and Deb had a doctor's
appointment that morning and needed me to go with her, so I decided I would. "Let's go do everything and we'll watch where I finished
on the five o'clock news," I told her. But she insisted I stay home
and made me promise to call her at the doctor's office if I heard
anything. Again, I expected that I'd hear from Jack Lang at 10:15
if I'd won, so when I hadn't by 10:40, I went out to the garage and
started doing some work. Ten minutes later, the phone rang and
when the caller asked for me, I knew who it was. He told me that
I'd won and gotten nineteen of the twenty-eight first-place votes
and congratulated me. When I hung up I did one of those Toyota

leaps before calling Deb, my mother, and brothers. As the day went along and I heard from teammates—Gedman, Don Baylor, Nipper, McNamara, Fischer—and friends, it was all a fantasy.

But in the seventy-two hours afterward, something seemed to be taken away by all the controversy. Don Mattingly said he didn't think a pitcher should win it over an everyday player. Well, if there were a most outstanding player, he would have won it, hands down. But I think unless there are unusual circumstances that the most valuable player has to be on the team that wins, and I'd told people all along that I'd have voted for Rice. In fact, Rice had bonuses of $150,000 for finishing first and $100,000 for finishing second in the balloting, and I'd told him that I'd start every interview stating that he should win it if he'd split the incentive with me and we'd laugh. I didn't even know at the time if I had any such incentive, and as it turned out, I got $25,000 for the Cy Young, nothing for the MVP. Who cares? The award's worth a lot more than money, but then I'd trade both awards in for the World Series ring. Then Henry Aaron called my election "a joke," and I got asked about that so often that when I was being inducted into my high school Hall of Fame at Spring Woods a few days later, I cracked, "My biggest regret is that Henry Aaron isn't still playing." It took away from the excitement at the time, but not for long.

Over the next few weeks, Alan was getting anywhere from five to thirty-five calls a day wanting me to do something. Commercials. Appearances. They wanted me to be at the Lombardi Dinner, where they gave the award for the top college football lineman in the country. The Bluebonnet Bowl people wanted me to toss the coin. I can see how the Cy Young Award jinx got started, because it's easy to try to do something every day. I told Alan that unless things work into my schedule—for instance, I'd be happy to do something when I go back to Boston for the writers' dinner—that I can't give the time. I've been running from the day I got home to Texas. I've been to a conditioning expert; I told him I wanted to put on seven pounds of upper body strength without losing any flexibility, and he gave me a squatting program with free weights that will build up my legs that I started on December 1. About the same time, I had to go back to my weights work for my shoulder, and by the first of the year I have to start throwing. All these endorsements and appearances are fine and I appreciate the attention, but I'm never going to be making my money in commercials. If I go 4–12 or even 12–12 next year, I won't hear from any of them again. My livelihood is throwing a baseball, the birth of Koby Aaron on December 4 is the most important personal thing in my life, and I'm not going to let outside income interfere with my priorities. I'm the first Boston pitcher to win the MVP and I'm the first starting pitcher since Vida Blue (1971) to win it; now I'd like to be the one who ends the Cy Young jinx. Oh yes. And win Boston's first Series since whenever it was.

·2·
LOOKING BACK TO GROWING UP

"I remember watching him pitch in Little League when he was nine. He struck out the side on nine pitches, and the catcher's glove made a popping noise. That's when I thought we had something special in the family."
— *Bess Wright,*
Roger's mother

WHEN ONE achieves some success and notoriety it's interesting how many people come out of the closets of the past to claim their share of that success. We've certainly experienced it. I constantly read where this person or that person was responsible for teaching me something vital on the road to Boston or that someone had predicted when I was sixteen that I was going to be a star; even my high school coach admits he never would have predicted it. My mother gets letters from people back in Ohio who want to get back in touch with her—most of them people who wanted nothing to do with us when we were there. When the Red Sox played in Detroit and Cleveland the second time around, I started getting calls from people claiming to be my relatives. This is all well and good, but my family sometimes takes offense. I had some strong influences in my high school and college days, but it was my family who pushed and molded my career. My story isn't one of a kid who was born with a silver spoon in his mouth or had the childhood talent of a prodigy for whom everything was natural. I know what got me to the big leagues and it's hard work; and because I know where I came from and how I got where I am now, I think I know that hard work and only hard work will keep me here. I made my own chances and I made my own breaks, and nobody gave me anything.

Not that I had a tough childhood. To the contrary, I feel as if I was almost spoiled, because I can't ever remember wanting for anything except possibly a father in the stands watching me pitch. Even then my stepfather was so wonderful to the whole family, my mother was such a stablizing force for my entire life, and my brother Randy watched out for me so well that that want was never a setback of any kind. Randy always said that because most of our lives were without any real father we had to stick together more closely than most families and take care of one another. We did a pretty good job.

I never knew my blood father, Bill Clemens. He was a driver for a chemical plant, and apparently he was on the road a lot. I was five months old when my mother picked up and left him, early in 1963. And as usual, she made the right decision. He was anti-sports and discouraged my oldest brother, Rick, from playing football, which he loved. Randy told me that my father would leave some money out in the morning as payment for a chore he wanted Randy to do, like cleaning the house. If Randy hadn't done the chore when he got home, he'd take Randy out to the barn. That was tough for Randy, too, because he was a great athlete and needed time to work out. Mom made sure he was encouraged, and she saved enough Top Value stamps to get him his first baseball glove. The only time I ever talked to my real dad was when I was ten. He called one night. I still don't know what reason he had to call, to hassle Mom or whatever. First I cut into him and then Randy cut into him, and he hung up on us. I told him that if I ever saw him around here it would be the last time he saw any of us, and he never came around. It's funny. When the Red Sox were in Cleveland this season, I got a couple of calls from people saying they were his relatives and wanted to get together, after all these years.

Five of us—Rick, Randy, Brenda, Janet, and I—were born before they split up. Then my mother married Woody Booher, whom I consider to be my father and who is my sister Bonnie's father. He was a tool-and-dye man and gave us everything we could have asked for. This past year we located and repurchased an old motorcycle of his, just so I could keep it as a remembrance. He was forever taking us on rides on that bike, Brenda or Janet on the rear, me in the front, and it meant so much to us that I repurchased his old cycle from a guy in Ohio this past year for $500.

I had been born in Dayton itself, in what Randy claims was a

tough side of town, but when Mom married Woody we moved out
to Vandalia. When I say I was spoiled, I mean it. I had everything
I ever wanted. Everything I asked for, I seemed to get. As far as
I was concerned, we had all the money in the world. It was a little
tougher on my brothers, but my remembrances were growing up
with Woody. We had a big house, a huge yard, a pool. We had a
big barn where we kept six horses, one for everyone in the family.
We had a buggy that would fit five people, and we'd go off on Christmas rides. I have a lot of great memories up there. When Woody
was alive, my mother didn't have to work. She just took care of
us. He was a remarkable man. I remember that he loved to watch
"Bonanza" every night, and how he used to tickle me with his
whiskers and bought me my first BB gun. He drove us around the
country so we could see things like the Grand Canyon. My mother
had a little Honda 90 motorcycle, too, and would take me to prac-
tices on it. Some people thought I was crazy when I jumped up
on the police horse in Fenway the afternoon the Red Sox clinched
the division, but I've been riding horses all my life. In fact, one
of the reasons Deb and I bought our house in Katy where we did
is that we both love to ride and it's right across the road from the
largest equestrian center in the country. Naturally, I also grew up
loving motorcycles, and had a lot of different bikes along the way.
I spent a lot of hours riding hills and trails on my dirt bike in Ohio.

I had a few select friends, but we tended to stick close together
as a family. My grandmother Myrta Lee lived around there, too.
She says she raised me, and she was a character. My mother wasn't
much for spankings, but Myrta Lee was a stickler for discipline.
When we went to her house and got into any sort of trouble, she'd
give us a beating. She'd tell whoever was in trouble to go out in
the backyard, break off a branch, and bring in a switch. I was no
dummy. I'd get the smallest branch in the world. She's something.
She's eighty-two and while she can't come to the games when we're
in Detroit, she watches them all on television.

Woody died of a heart attack when I was nine. He got up from
the dinner table and went up to the bedroom. I didn't know what
happened, but one of my older sisters took Bonnie—who was five—
and me to the basement. When we saw the red lights outside, we
knew something had happened, even if we didn't fully understand
what was going on. His death was tough for all of us, for he was
such a great man and worked very hard to make us all happy. He

left us that house and quite a bit of money; for the next three years after he died in 1971, we were getting the move to Texas in place, and he certainly made it possible.

The other really difficult time I remember as a kid was before Woody died, when Rick found out he had to go to Vietnam. I was seven or eight, and I remember after dinner one night we were watching one number after another come up on the TV. I didn't know what was going on, but of course they were the birth dates that dictated who would be chosen in the draft lottery. All of a sudden my mother let out a scream, and everyone broke into tears. I was too young to comprehend, but Rick's number had come up and they all knew that he was on his way to Vietnam. The next four days were really bad, as he prepared to go. It makes me realize that I was lucky not to have to go through all that, now, and how glad I am to have been born after the entire Vietnam experience. It affected his life a little bit, for he had to make an adjustment reentering into regular civilization when he came home, an adjustment that at first wasn't easy. He's like a lot of people with nightmares of that place. He doesn't like those Rambo movies, or anything like that. He won't watch them or talk about them. But he's fine now, and very attached to the family. We've become close, and if anyone ever tried to physically hurt me or rob my house, somebody would have to kill him. He's not crazy, but if anyone did anything to the family, someone would think he was, especially with his big Harley that he loves to ride. He'd go get someone. That's the way he is. That's the way our family is. One of the reasons I've been so adamant about a wives' room and security at Fenway is that if anything happened to Deb, I'd go right up off the field, for my family's more important than my pitching.

While I was growing up, Randy was the star as far as I was concerned. As I got older, I realized how great an athlete he really was. He still holds records there in Vandalia. He was all-state, all-everything as a basketball guard, and once I got old enough, it was brother, brother, brother. "You'll never be as good as your brother," I heard for years. He used to take me along to his baseball games and let me be the batboy. He also made sure that I got the right kind of competition in Little League. I always loved baseball. My mother says she thought she had something when I was nine and one day I struck out the side on nine pitches. Randy said he could start to tell that I had some talent about the same time, but he helped by getting me into leagues against older kids. But at that time he was the athlete I looked up to. Randy had to have boxes stacked up in the cellar for his clippings and his trophies. Out of high school, he went to Bethel College in Indiana. He was tearing that up, and friends told him he should go to a higher level, and he got recruited to Mississippi College. It didn't take long for him to shine there, either. He waited his turn, playing a couple of minutes in their first two games, but he played so well he quickly took one of the regular guards' positions and went on from there. We used to fly down to see him a lot, and when he graduated he had two chances for tryouts. One was with New Orleans, the other with the Celtics, and the only one he had time to make was in New Orleans, which didn't work out. He and his wife, Kathy, had a baby. She was teaching and they followed Rick's lead and moved to Houston, where he finished his degree at Houston Baptist. Eventually, Randy went back to Mississippi and was an assistant, and then they moved to Ohio to be near Kathy's parents. He had a high school head coaching job at Troy, where he was 45–8 in 1983 and 1984, before setting out to try to get a college assistant job. It's a shame that he hasn't gotten a break yet, because he'd be an outstanding coach on any level.

But back in the early 1970s, Rick had already been calling us in Ohio saying that the economy was booming in Houston and we should move down there. By the time Randy moved there, I was in the ninth grade. I went down and lived with Randy in 1976 and spent that year—which was my final junior high year in Ohio—going back and forth between Houston and Vandalia. Kathy was teaching, and she really disciplined me in terms of applying myself to academics. My mother moved down for good the next year, and we lived in Sugartown at first, so I spent my sophomore year at Dulles High School, which at the time was the biggest high school in Texas—so big that as a kid from what seemed like a small town in Ohio, I was intimidated. I played the first few games on the JV, then I got called up to the varsity and finished 12–1. I thought I was a hot shot, but Randy said, "You're not getting enough competition here. We're going to have to go to a better school and see what you can do." Randy had already been looking around and that spring took me to a regional tournament game between Spring Woods and Bellaire. Randy said that they were the two best teams around at the time, that both coaches were excellent. "We'll watch this seven-inning game and when it's over I want you to tell me which school you want to go to," he told me. Spring Woods lost 4–2 and Randy thought I'd say Bellaire, but I chose Spring Woods. We picked up as a family and moved over into the Spring Woods District.

To that point, I'd always been a pitcher, but I'd also played third, short, first, and caught. Because my birthday is in August, I could cross more age limits and play in different leagues, so usually I was in three at the same time. The summer before my junior year I was playing for the Legion Post team—which won the state championship—as well as the Katy League, Carl Young, and Houston Big League. I might have ten games a week. I'd start a couple, relieve in a couple, and play both shortstop or first base as well. When I signed up with some teams, I'd just sign up as a shortstop, but they caught on when I played the other leagues because they'd read it in the papers. Eventually, I'd begin to have conflicts.

It wasn't as if I walked into Spring Woods and was handed anything. When I got there, I was the third string pitcher. I was a sixteen-year-old junior, and they already had two outstanding senior pitchers in Rick Luecken and Raymer Noble. At that point, I wasn't close to completing growing. I was playing defensive end in the fall and had to bulk up to 220, then get down for baseball; and they said I still had baby fat. I guess I was 6'1" or 6'2" and between 200 and 205 pounds, and I hadn't reached my full velocity. I thought I threw somewhere in the mid-eighties, although there are people who claim I was more consistently around 80 miles per hour. Luecken threw 90–91, Noble was 86–87, and they were outstanding. Luecken went on to Texas A&M and was in the Seattle organization until being traded to Kansas City this past winter, and after doing everything at the University of Houston, Noble has been in the Astros system. Noble did absolutely everything at Houston—pitch, play short—and is one of those guys who loves to play and can find a way to win. It seems as if the peaks of their careers came early, although I still think that given the right opportunity, either one could still make the big leagues. That year we had a team of almost all seniors and only four of us juniors, and we were 31–4 and got to the state quarterfinals. I tried to take advantage of every opportunity I could get. I broke the school strikeout record with eighteen. The league record was nineteen, set by Westminster High

School's David Clyde against Spring Woods in 1973. The first guy bunted his way on in Clyde's game, the next batter hit into a double play, and he punched out the last nineteen. My coach at Spring Woods, Charlie Maiorana, always said that if he'd coached Clyde, he'd have known he had a big leaguer on his hands. With me, he didn't have any idea. He says I was an oversize, pear-shaped kid with fat cheeks and that I looked very young. We had as many as thirty-nine scouts at almost every one of our games because of Luecken and Noble, and Coach Maiorana remembers that when they were all there to see Craig James—who was the big hitter for Stratford—my eyes lit up when Luecken struck him out three times. My next start was the eighteen-strikeout game, and later I pitched at Stratford and struck out James three times as well.

At Spring Woods—as well as at San Jacinto Junior College and the University of Texas—I was fortunate to have coaches who were strong, positive influences on me. Charlie Maiorana was a tremendous disciplinarian. It was under him that I learned so much about taking care of my body. We'd run the line-to-lines every day, hour after hour. We lived about two miles from the high school, and almost every day after practice I'd put my books and clothes in a napsack and run home. Coach Maiorana's wife, Sandy, is living testimony to all he taught and believed in. She's the oldest person in the world with cystic fibrosis and has battled and fought against all odds all her life as an example to all of us who are a lot more fortunate. Charlie would take Sandy to the Texas Institute for Rehabilitation in Houston, and he'd always be moved. "How come kids take so much for granted?" he'd ask. "They don't realize that there are people who would give anything to breathe without an iron lung. To some, a sunset is the thrill of each day." He normally took each one of his classes to that hospital. Ours never went. He said that ours was the most mature class he'd ever had. That means a lot, coming from him. Work habits have had a significant bearing on getting me to the big leagues. In my home and in the programs I played in, I was taught to believe that how I live my life has a bearing on success. I agreed to have a drug-testing clause put in my contract with the Red Sox because I wanted to say, "Look, this is the way I take care of myself and live, it should be worth something to you." Especially when I see some of the things that go on.

Coach Maiorana also taught me a lot about the art of pitching. I played football under him, as he was the defensive coordinator, and given the nature of Texas football faced some outstanding players such as James, Rich Luck, and Doug Dawson. I actually got a few inquiries and scholarship offers for football as a defensive end, from places like North Texas State, Northeastern Louisiana, and even Georgia the year that Herschel Walker was going there. None of the offers were the kinds of things James got at SMU and once baseball season began approaching I guess they figured that's where I was headed, so they backed off. But there was no question about my first love being baseball. Maiorana has an uncanny ability to pick out certain character traits and exploit them. It's my nature to react to anything that makes me want to *prove* something, and he could get on me about my weight or about my ability to win big games.

Coach Maiorana was a superb coach in terms of the fundamentals of mechanics. He was a great believer in simulation, where we'd go into the gym without baseballs and work on nothing but our throwing motion. I still believe in that. I'll simulate in front of mirrors in the clubhouse or at home, just to get the proper mechanics rolling. I also had started learning a lot of things for myself. I read a book or two on conditioning, which suggested keeping a diary to help determine my best playing weight. I began to find that I pitched best at a certain weight around 200, and if I got 3 or 4 pounds over that, I didn't pitch as well. I also read a couple of books and watched an old film on pitching that taught me about stages of a pitch. It was then that I broke my motion into six stages. The first two are the rock and momentum. The third finishes the first half through the break of the hands; then four, five, and six bring you to the plate with the rolling motion of the glove. In that film, they put a rope around the pitcher and made him fall right toward the catcher so he'd drive to throw it right through him, which is what I learned to do. My six stages of the delivery are things I assembled myself from what others had taught me, and I still follow them. I'd watched Tom Seaver and Nolan Ryan so carefully all my life that I wasn't surprised when Seaver concurred with them entirely.

My senior year turned out to be a lot of fun. I went 13–5 and we went to the regionals, but while I heard from eleven different schools, I wasn't getting big scholarship offers. The best I probably could have gotten from Texas was a half-scholarship. I was a seventeen-year-old senior, and after my mother, Randy, and I sat down and talked about it, we decided it would be a good idea to stay around home for a year. I had offers from San Jac and Blinn (in Brenham), and we knew of Coach Wayne Graham's reputation at San Jacinto Junior College. So it was a simple decision that wasn't exactly clouded by an offer from the Twins. Their scout came to see me twice at the high school field. I hadn't been drafted, but he was offering me a chance to play professional baseball. Finally, he came to the house and told me, "If you don't sign now, you'll never get the chance to play again." After the football season, one night I had run down to the high school field, lay on the mound, and thought about what I wanted to do. Sure, I dreamed about professional baseball, but it wasn't foremost in my mind. I was thinking about what I'd do after I graduated and what I could get my family for Christmas presents. But when I heard what the Twins' scout said, I was very upset. My mother threw him out of the house and yelled, "Don't let the door hit you in the behind on the way out." I wasn't convinced. I went upstairs and closeted myself in my room for two days. The famous Phillies scout Don Gassaway (now with the Texas Rangers) also talked to us and offered me somewhere around $1500, but as he was telling us that I'd go start in the Appalachian League, my mother told him, "He already knows how to ride buses."

My mother was right, just as she had been when she made the decision to move us to Houston. San Jacinto College turned out to be the right place for me, as well.

My coach there, Wayne Graham, is a workaholic. He played professionally for ten years, played a little for the Phillies and Mets in 1964 and 1965, and has won three national championships in four years and more than 80 percent of his games at San Jac. He was coaching at Spring Branch High in Houston my senior year when he saw me at Spring Woods. He knew at the time that he was moving on to San Jac, and he made it clear that he wanted me to pitch for him. He said he "loved them strikes," and later told people that while he realized the knock on me was that I didn't throw hard enough, he knew it was correctable. When I got there in 1980, he told me that I wasn't finishing through, that I was trying to do everything with my body. He kept saying "finish strong," and he did a lot of yelling at me, but he also kept reminding me that I was only eighteen. He chewed me out a few times for bad pitches, and he could really chew people out. But he taught me a lot about pitching. That's when I began blowing the ball. I was going through growing pains, filling out and growing from 6'2" to close to 6'4", but it started coming together. He says I was throwing about 82 mph when I arrived there that fall. He got me to let it go and air it out as hard as I could, and by the spring I was up at 90 and 91, and I remember the day that the assistant coach Paul Miller told me after a game that I'd broken 90 for the first time. He told me that I had "genius-level control," and he kept telling me that not many people have it. "It's the perfection of coordination and mechanics," he said. "Not many people have it. I saw Don Sutton when he was with the Astros, and he had it. And so do you." [The numbers at Spring Woods were 112 strikeouts and 24 walks in 108 innings, 82 strikeouts and 38 walks in 85⅔ innings at San Jacinto College North.]

San Jac was a good growing experience, both in terms of pitching and maturity. Graham calls that period in my baseball life "a crossroads," and I clearly was on the right road. It was fun, too. I finished 9–2, and we lost in the final game before the junior college world series, when I gave up a tenth-inning homer and lost 3–2 to San Jacinto-McLennan. Graham was a tough, fair disciplinarian. One day we were in this van way out in the sticks going to Dee County, and he warned a couple of players in the back to stop fooling around. They didn't stop, so he pulled the van over to the side of the road, opened the door, and told the three guys to get out. I got out, too, to let them out, only he slammed the door shut and took off. He *thought* we were only about a quarter of a mile from the field, because up ahead there were some lights that looked like a ballpark.

They turned out to be rodeo lights, and there we were, in 95-degree heat, the sun at its peak. We had to climb over fences, walk through yards and cactus and dirt. One farmer thought we were prowlers and fired warning shots over our heads. Finally, after about four miles and an hour and a half, we found the ballpark. When we climbed over the outfield fence and jumped onto the field, we got a standing ovation from both our teammates and the crowd. That also turned out to be the closest I ever came to a no-hitter—two outs in the bottom of the ninth before I gave up a hit.

As the season wore on, I was blowing the ball by hitters, and Randy and I sat down to discuss my future. As much as San Jac had helped me, he felt that I needed to move on to the next level of competition and get my tail kicked around a little. So we looked around at big-time schools. I heard from Arkansas, but the first school I went to visit was Baylor. While I was visiting there, I was getting calls from other colleges in my motel room. LSU was one, and a couple of other Southeastern Conference schools. When I got home, I received letters from Oklahoma State and Arizona, but by then Coach Graham had let Coach Cliff Gustafson at the University of Texas know that I was leaving junior college after just one year. Coach Gus had said that, while my numbers at Spring Woods were impressive, I was "very mediocre." Within a year, I'd changed his opinion.

In any event, Coach Gustafson did call me and said that he heard that I was interested in moving on and that he was interested in giving me a scholarship. He told me I should come up to Austin and see the field and the facility. That wasn't necessary, since every year we'd go to Austin for the state championship, but I wanted to make the visit anyway. It wasn't as if I was jumping ship on Coach Graham and San Jac, because the scholarship there was for one year. Anyway, any kid from Texas who had a chance to be a Longhorn would jump at the opportunity. I got there in the morning, met Coach Gus, and toured the facility. He didn't go to lunch with me. *Nothing* could break his lunch routine. He's had the same lunch every day for more than twenty years: peanut butter and honey, a bag of chips, and iced tea with lemon. Every day. Every other day, he goes out on the field and runs two miles; but Coach Gus doesn't jog, he runs six-minute miles, and no one — no matter how much he wants him — is going to break that routine.

After an assistant coach took me to lunch at the Filling Station, one of the most popular spots around there, I went over to the School of Business Administration, went over my transcript, and was told there was no problem with my admission or transfer of credits. When I got back to Gus's office, he had the scholarship all typed up, ready for me to sign. I told him my mother had to be present for me to sign, which was true. Then he asked me for an oral commitment. I told him I couldn't, yet. "OK, if you're leaving at 6:00, you'll be home in Houston by 8:30, I'll expect a call at 8:40 with a decision," he told me. "Read these papers on the ride." He handed me the scholarship form.

I stopped for gas or got something to eat on the way home and was about 15 minutes late, and when I walked in the door at 8:45, my mother was on the phone. "Coach Gustafson wants to talk to you," she said, and handed me the phone.

"Is it in the mail yet?" was his first question.

"No, sir."

"Well, don't you want to be a Longhorn?"

"Yes, sir. Everyone wants to be a Longhorn." There was no harm in buttering him up a little now that he knew my decision.

I then told him there was one hitch. If I gave him an oral commitment, I wanted one back in return. I told him I wanted the ball in the nationally televised opener at Miami, and I wanted the ball in the home opener against Texas A&M. He told me I had the ball both nights. That was that. I was a Longhorn.

Problem is, while I was talking to Coach Gus, I got another call on call waiting from Mickey Sullivan at Baylor, so I had to keep him on hold while I finished with Gustafson. When I got back to Sullivan, whom I liked very much, I had to tell him I was going to Texas. "Go ahead," he said, obviously upset with me. "You'll never pitch. You'll sit around like the rest of those blue-chippers." I thought from that point on that I should always tell someone like that that I'm not going to do what he wanted, just to see the reaction. I've always wondered what Gustafson would have done had I told him I was going to Baylor, but he's so honest, I don't think he'd have been any different. Coach Gus may be a lot of things, but he is honest, he is sincere, and he should be doing an E. F. Hutton commercial, because when he speaks, people listen.

But as I started playing in the summer leagues in 1981, I was drafted by the Mets in the twelfth round. Their scout, Jim Terrell, had actually been told by his bosses to try to sign me before the draft — which they could do since I was in junior college at the time — for $7500; but he told them I wouldn't consider that figure. He liked me so much that he was willing to put up $7500 of his own money that he'd received in a pension upon retirement from the telephone company. When he told the Mets' scouting and player development director, Joe McIlvaine, of his unique offer, McIlvaine doubled their offer to $15,000. But I wasn't signing for that, and they selected me in the twelfth round of the draft. Right after the draft, the Mets were in town, so they asked me to come to the Dome to work out. I was really excited. I used to love to go to the Dome and sit down by the bull pen when Nolan Ryan or Joe Sambito was warming up. I loved the sound that their fastballs made in the catchers' gloves. Since the place was usually pretty empty, it sounded like guns going off. Now that he's my teammate, Joe doesn't like to hear that stuff, or how I used to wait outside the parking lot when he and Nolan would come out to their cars or how my girlfriend used to sleep in a Joe Sambito uniform top. He shouldn't get too upset, though. When Tom Seaver came over from the White Sox, Joe told everyone that he wrote his senior high school English thesis on Seaver and the Miracle Mets.

I put on the Mets uniform, went to the bull pen, and threw for them. Tim Leary—who then had some arm trouble and, ironically, beat us three times for the Brewers in 1986—was throwing right next to me. Joe Torre was the manager, and he and Bob Gibson watched me; after I heard a couple of comments, they went down to the dugout and watched from there. I guess Gibson wasn't impressed. I thought I was throwing the ball pretty well, and Coach Graham, who threw batting practice for the Astros that day, said that I looked very good in a Mets uniform. But it all worked out for the best, and anyway, when I struck out twenty this past April for the Red Sox, Gibson said he'd never heard of me. Not that the Mets gave up right then. They came very close to signing me.

They sent one of their top cross-checkers, Harry Minor, in to watch me after the draft to try to decide how much money I was worth. I was pitching in three or four leagues at the time, and the night he came to see me, I was throwing my second complete game in thirty-six hours—the third of four starts in seven days—and didn't have much. Later, when Minor was doing some advance scout work during the World Series in 1986, he admitted that he had told McIlvaine that he recommended that they offer me no more than $10,000. But Terrell insisted I was better than that, so McIlvaine flew down. The first weekend he came, both days' games were rained out and he had to fly home. The same thing the next weekend, so he never saw me. The difference with the Mets was the equivalent of my last year in school and what my dad had left me. (A clause in the will stipulated payments would stop if I received other income.) They were offering $30,000, and I wanted my last year of school—around $6000—and the money that my mother mailed me, about $650 a month for the school year that had been left by my stepfather. If I signed, I'd have lost that. They didn't realize what values meant to me. My father had left that for me—three years of school, money I'd have lost. I wanted it to go to my mother, and she could have used the $8000 or $9000 for my sister while I was off in A ball.

McIlvaine and Terrell trapped me off in the parking lot after I'd struck out fourteen in a Carl Young game in the Houston City League a few days after they'd made the original offer. They put a briefcase on the top of the car and tried to talk me into signing. I told them that my mother needed to be present; anyway, it sounds great but they didn't realize how much what my father left meant to me. If they'd have come up with that money I thought my family had coming, I'd be in the Mets organization today. I'll never forget how nice Jim Terrell was, and I appreciate how much he believed in me. Later in the summer, he came by and saw me work out at Spring Woods. He asked me if my price was the same. I told him yes. I later found out that he called back to New York, and he had argued them to a difference of $5000. He made his final case to Lou Gorman, who was then the vice president of baseball operations, and Gorman decided that what I wanted was too much. How ironic. When I got to the major leagues less than three years later, Gorman was general manager of the Red Sox. When I was pitching against the Mets in the World Series, Terrell said that he didn't realize that Gorman was clairvoyant.

So, in the fall of 1981, I was off to Austin, which turned out to be a great experience and another right decision. Yes, Coach Gus kept his word. The series at Miami was canceled, but he gave me the ball against Texas A&M, and I dominated. Luecken and I kept trying to match up, but it never worked out.

No one can ever underestimate the Texas baseball tradition as far as I'm concerned. The first time I saw that sign that read "The Texas Tradition Will Not Be Entrusted to the Timid or the Weak," I was moved. No other program has won as many games in its history as the more than twenty-two hundred in Longhorn history. They have been to Omaha for the college world series more times— twenty-five—than any other school, and thirteen of those have come in Gustafson's twenty years. They've averaged sixty wins a year for the last eight seasons—fifty a year under Gustafson— won fifty-nine of seventy-one Southwest Conference titles, made it to Omaha six straight times, and won it four times. Some complain about the pressure, but it prepares you for a competitive business and world. There are so many outstanding players at Texas that if you sit, you might not get another chance to play. Most of the guys on the bench could start for almost all the other Southwest Conference schools, and it's a strong baseball league from top to bottom. Losing, very simply, isn't tolerated; and day after day after day, it is impressed on you that you'd better be aggressive or you won't be playing for long. How good was the talent? Nine guys off the '82 team were drafted, seven off the '83 club.

I actually had a better season as a sophomore than as a junior. I was 15–2, and we finished second in the college world series. Calvin (Schiraldi), Mike (Capel), and I became very close friends. At first, there was a strong sense of rivalry. They were both all-staters in high school, I was second team, and we were competing to be the top dog at Texas. But as we got to know one another, we became very close friends—both Cal and Mike were in my wedding—and the competition became a positive thing. If Mike won, then I wanted to pitch better than he did; and if I succeeded, Cal wanted to do the same.

I lost the final college world series game 2–1 to Miami on two unearned runs, and I'll never forget that afterward we were all out in the parking lot saying our good-byes to Spike Owen. He was the person I most looked up to at Texas, one of those rare people who somehow made everyone around him positive at all times. Coach Gus always said that he was the most popular player ever at Texas, and that's because people there loved the way he played the game. He went at it hard all the time, always aggressive, and everyone who ever saw him knew that he loved every second he was on the field. He always has that little smile on his face, an expression that some major leaguers don't like when they don't realize it's sincere. He was a vacuum cleaner at shortstop. I'd just hope that if I didn't strike someone out that the ball would get hit to Spike, because he made every play he had to make. The Texas Winning Tradition was embodied in Spike Owen.

Anyway, Spike had been drafted in the first round by the Mariners, and he was getting ready to start his new life, and I couldn't stop myself from crying. I was sure that we could never be the same without him, that we'd never have a chance to win the series in 1983, and I was sad because I thought I would never again play with Spike.

When we came back as juniors in 1982, we seemingly were picked by everyone to win it all. Calvin, Mike, Kirk Killingsworth and I were the returning pitchers, and we were on almost every college baseball magazine cover. We all had nicknames. I was Goose, because I was built a little like Gossage, and they even gave me a Yankee hat. It's funny now that Spike and I are back playing with each other that while everyone else calls me Rocket or Rog, I still hear him hollering "Come on, Goose" out at shortstop. Cal was Nibbler because he could throw that slider down and away on the corner all day long. Mike was Gamer, and Kirk was the Killer; he was a killer coming out of the bull pen. That really was a good team. Mike Brumley (later of the Cubs) moved in from center field to shortstop. Jeff Hearon (later of Toronto) was the catcher. Jose Tolentino (Oakland) was the first baseman. Billy Bates (the Brewers) was the second baseman. We even had younger pitchers such as Bruce Ruffin, who had such a great year for the Phillies in 1986, as well as Philadelphia prospect Eric Boudreaux and Cleveland's Mike Poehl.

What happened was that we went out and got off to a start that was as bad as any decent team could have had. I went out and got knocked around a couple of times. Calvin got rapped around a little. Mike had a couple of no-decisions. Finally Coach Gus stomped into the locker room one day and shouted, "Go in and reread all those articles about yourselves." The slump didn't last, although I had one late in the season. I've been fortunate enough to play in a number of pressure situations, but I think a player's draft year presents a unique pressure. Joe Ford, who scouts for Toronto, says he doesn't like to make any judgment on a college player in his junior year, and I'm grateful to Danny Doyle of the Red Sox that he felt the same way. I didn't know Doyle. Like some of those other great veteran Boston scouts like George Digby and Joe Stephenson, Doyle is a loner who listens only to his own judgment. So many of those guys sit together, talk together, and all form the same opinions. That season it got to the point that it was disconcerting to see forty radar guns poised on my every pitch. Then, too, there were rumors all over the place about me. I don't hold it against Gustafson, but he wanted me to stay another year, and some of the scouts that were close to him started spreading rumors about me: that I didn't maintain my velocity more than five or six innings, that I wasn't tough. . . . Never mind that I was pitching nine innings on Friday nights, then coming back and pitching in relief the next day. Then I got frustrated by it all, and I had some disagreements with pitches being called from the bench, and it all came to a head. I lost a couple of games, I got knocked out in a tournament game, tore my uniform off, and needed to get things back together. I finished 13–5, 3.04 with 22 walks and 151 strikeouts in 166 innings. Calvin was 14–2, 1.74, and was the Baseball America College Pitcher of the Year. Capel was 13–1, 2.98; and Killingsworth was 12–3, 2.56.

I did get things back together in the regionals against Mississippi State, which had Rafael Palmeiro (now of the Cubs), Will Clark (the Giants), and Bobby Thigpen (the White Sox) in the middle of the order. By then, some clubs had backed off, but Doyle kept telling the Red Sox that I was his man and that they should draft me. We won the regionals and went to Omaha, where I waited for the draft the day I was supposed to pitch against Oklahoma State. Calvin, Brumley, and I all had heard that we could go in the first round; and Hearon, Tolentino, and Capel expected to go high, so it was a big day. Hearon drove me crazy, continually calling my room pretending to be from some team. Tim Belcher of Mount Vernon Nazarene College was the top pick in the draft, by Minnesota. I knew the Twins wouldn't take me. I thought my first chance was Texas in the third spot, but they took shortstop Jeff Kunkel of Rider College. Then I thought that Houston might take me with the eighth selection, but they took catcher Robbie Wine of Oklahoma State. Instead, I stayed until the nineteenth selection and the Red Sox, and when I got a call from a newspaperman telling me I'd been selected by Boston, I was completely surprised. As far as I was concerned, Boston was a foreign country. It worked out perfectly, of course, but at the time I wondered a little about being drafted behind so many guys I'd played against, like Stan Hilton (Baylor right-hander, the fifth pick by Oakland), Darrell Ackerfelds (former Arkansas right-hander, the seventh pick by Seattle), Wine (eighth pick by Houston), Ray Hayward (Oklahoma left-hander, the tenth selection by San Diego), and Erik Sonberg (Wichita State left-hander, selected eighteenth by Los Angeles), but as I learned later, rumors are a big part of the draft. The Texas Rangers people told Doyle at the end of the college world series that I couldn't hold my velocity past the fifth or sixth inning, right after watching the final game, where I struck out five in the last two innings. The great part of that draft was that Mike (Pup) Brumley was taken by the Red Sox with their special compensation pick at the beginning of the second round. The ironies were that Doyle and Eddie Kasko, the scouting director, now say they might well have taken Calvin had I been selected come their turn, and while Brumley was traded the next May to the Cubs in the Dennis Eckersley–Buckner deal, we all ended up with Spike in 1986. Look what happened. Now I wish they'd go get Hearon from Toronto, Capel from the Cubs, Ruffin. . . . (Incidentally, Capel was selected by the Cubs on the thirteenth round, Killingsworth by Texas on the seventh, and Schiraldi was the twenty-ninth selection, by the Mets.)

Calvin had beaten James Madison 12–0 in the opener of the college world series. The draft started the next day, and I had to pitch that night and had a relatively easy game beating Oklahoma State 9–1. Actually, there's no such thing as an easy game with those guys because the rivalry is so great. The year before, when we played them in Omaha, ESPN had to do away with the dugout microphones. Brumley was on first in that game and kept telling Jim Traber (now with Baltimore), "Everybody hates you, even your teammates." And they started shoving each other. Traber threw a rolling block on our second baseman, Calvin went at him, and I went at it with Wine. As I found out later, not all of the players are so hostile; one of their outfielders, Scott Wade, is in the Boston organization and a terrific person. On the field, though, they came across as the renegades of college baseball. That's all the nature of big-time college baseball, for I found I, too, really let my emotions fly.

Even though I was thinking about moving on to my professional career, I still was completely caught up in that series week. First, the people there in Omaha are great. They love that baseball, they pack the ballpark every night, they put on dinners and spreads, and they even take care of you at the local track (for those who want to lose some money). Also, winning the 1983 college world series for Texas was something we had set our minds to since the previous June, and when I got my next start, Calvin—who was named the series MVP as well as the Baseball America College Pitcher of the Year—had gotten us within one final victory. I had to beat Alabama, which had Lou Piniella's cousin Dave Magadan, who I wish had succeeded Ray Knight as the Mets' third baseman one year earlier. He hit something like .560 that season. He was like Boggs. He got hits in his first nine series at bats, with a few walks thrown in. He struck out only six times all season, although Cal and I each got him twice. He also got us, however. He homered off Nibbler when he beat them, then he hit a chalk line, opposite field double to knock in two runs off me for an early 2–0 lead in that final game. But in the seventh inning, Brumley singled to start a two-run rally that Tolentino finished with a run-scoring bunt single, and I got stronger at the end of the 4–3 victory.

Unfortunately, there was a little controversy at the end. When I got the second-to-last out, the guy I struck out was yelling, "You're not number one, you ———, you ain't no number one pick," and it was pretty bad. Then when I got the final strikeout, I was just about to hug Calvin when this guy was still yelling at me near the mound. "Oh-for-three, take a seat, Meat," I yelled at him, and pointed upward. It came out over ESPN and somehow the whole thing got misunderstood. Some viewers thought I was cursing God, and oh, did I heard about it. Anyone who knows me realizes that I am a strong Christian who gives testimony and has strong beliefs; I just don't use baseball as a forum to preach. That was unfortunate, because it was the only blemish on an otherwise great week that brought the championship to Texas and bade my good-bye to my amateur baseball days.

·3·
FROM THE FARM
TO FENWAY

"One reason John McNamara is a good pitchers'
manager is that he never subscribes to that 'you have
to learn to pitch with pain' adage. That's what they
told Don Aase in California, and he needed three
separate operations. I've seen a lot of careers ruined
by managers and coaches making judgments about
a player's pain. Roger is fortunate that Mac cares
more about his pitching future than his
own managerial future."
— Bruce Kison,
Former Red Sox pitcher

So, IN THE spring of 1983,
life seemed pretty good: I'd come from the University of Texas, with
the carpets in the locker rooms and that park that was like a miniature Royals Stadium and the college world series with the jammed
ballpark and noise.

And found myself in Winter Haven with the Red Sox' A team.
"What am I doing here?" I asked myself. There were fifty people
in the stands, tops, which at least enabled you to identify whoever
was yelling at you. There were bugs everywhere. It rained every
day. One night Jeff Ledbetter (a former first-round draft pick out
of Florida State) almost got hit in the head with a fish. A bird had
plucked it out of Lake Lulu and was carrying it back to its nest
atop one of the towers in center field. The bird couldn't make it,
let go, and it just missed Ledbetter's head at first base. There were
gills flying everywhere.

I had wanted to start in AA, for I felt that the level of competition
that Texas had faced—especially in the regionals and the world
series—was pretty close to A level, but Ed Kenney feels that players
should start lower, have success, and earn their way up. It certainly

was different, although I hadn't known exactly what to expect. I signed with Boston for $121,000 after the college world series, then took a few days to recover from the mental exhaustion. Mr. Kenney was very nice about it, and told me to report to Winter Haven as soon as I was ready.

As bad as Winter Haven was, I'm actually lucky that I didn't end up with the Sox' other A League team in Winston-Salem, because I found out that if I'd been sent there they would have made me a reliever after a couple of starts. I didn't realize that the Goose business had turned up on Coach Joe Morgan's scouting report and that he compared me to Gossage. One of the things Randy had asked when negotiating my contract was whether there was a pitching coach on every level of the Boston farm system. He was told there was, which wasn't entirely true because they called Doug Camilli a pitching coach. He was actually a catcher and the coach working with the manager, Tom Kotchman. It's fortunate that I didn't get my mechanics out of whack in some way.

Their idea of discipline at Winter Haven was making sure that everyone showed the proper number of stripes on his socks, which I thought was silly. Then I got into some trouble for running. I thought the amount of running they did each day was a joke, so I did my 2 to 2½ miles and extra 60-yard sprints each day, usually early. "You can't do that, you do your running with everyone else, period," Tom Kotchman said. I was told to stop. I called Randy, and he finally had to call Mr. Kenney and get the thing worked out so I could condition myself the way I felt necessary. The one thing I learned right away is that there are a lot of players on that level who are complacent. Guys act like, "Hey, I'm getting paid, I'm a pro ballplayer, this is great, I'm great, and I'll automatically move up the level to The Show." Of course, it doesn't work that way. The Red Sox are unbelievably patient, too. They'll give players three and four chances. As far as I was concerned, I wanted to get in and out of Winter Haven—and the minors, for that matter—as quickly as possible.

Brumley went to Winter Haven with me, which was great. Things fell into place pretty well there, too. I made four starts, and after going five innings in my debut, completed the final three, allowing four runs, walking none, and striking out thirty-six in twenty-nine innings. I almost got into some trouble because of Pup (Brumley), however. We were playing the Lakeland Tigers this one night, and they had a bunch of older, big DH types. This one guy went way out of the baseline, threw a rolling block on Brumley, and hurt him. Now, if that's all he'd done, we'd have been upset enough, but when he got back to the bench he and a lot of the other players were laughing, making the Hook 'em Horns signs and yelling "Hook 'em Horns, Hook 'em Horns." I started the next night, and I struck out the first six batters. Then that guy who had hurt Brumley was batting seventh. What I wanted to do was tuck the ball inside and make him hit the dirt. I started it out inside and at his belt, but the ball exploded, ran up and in, and hit him right in the head. Well, I knew something would break out, so I charged the plate in case he was going to get up and want a piece of me, but when I got there he started to get up, then collapsed. I struck out fifteen, finished a shutout, and after the game Mr. Kenney told me I was going to AA in New Britain. He said that they had thought about sending me to AAA, in Pawtucket, but that the Pawtucket club was losing and New Britain had a good shot at making the Eastern League play-offs. So I burned up the telephone lines all night calling everyone to tell them I was headed for AA, and the next day I was en route to New England for the first time in my life, in July of 1983.

That turned out to be the right place to go, too. We had a great bunch of guys on that team: Pat Dodson at first, Steve Lyons at third, Kevin Romine in the outfield, Gary Miller-Jones at second, and Dave Malpeso catching. They'd battled all season to have a chance at the play-offs, and in the five weeks I was there, I got seven starts and got to be part of a team that really worked to make itself something. We faced Reading—who'd gone 96–44 during the regular season—in the first round of the play-offs and beat them. Rac Slider, our manager, tapped me for the opener, and when I was warming up, a funny thing happened. The home plate umpire came out and told me that I couldn't use my glove because there was Magic Marker scratched all over it. Now, I'll admit that there was. Back in college, some of the Texas girls had snuck into the clubhouse and, thinking that glove wasn't my gamer, scribbled a few things like "good luck, Goose" and "we love you" over it, and I had to cover it up. What bothered me was that this same umpire had been behind the plate for three or four of my previous starts, but because the Reading manager, Bill Dancy, was trying to interrupt my concentration, the ump went along with it and told me I couldn't use it. I said, "OK, I'll change it," and went back to completing my warm-ups. The umpire was mad because our dugout was jeering him, and all of a sudden he started cussing me. "You change that glove when I tell you, you ———," he was screaming. I had to be restrained, Rac had to be restrained, other players were out on the field, and there was all sorts of trouble. However, I realized what was at stake, calmed down, went out to the bull pen, and asked Charlie Mitchell (our ace reliever) for his glove. I started my warm-ups over, pitched eight shutout innings before allowing a run in the ninth, allowed three hits, no runs, walked two, struck out fifteen, and when it was over Dancy said that there was no way I should only be in that league. I appreciated that, but more important, we won the best-out-of-three series when Romine knocked in four runs in the 7–6 finale.

We then went on to play the Lynn Pirates in a best-of-five series. We were already up two to one when I got to start, and I threw a three-hitter and struck out ten. We won, 6–0. It was a great feeling to be on the mound for two championships in less than three months, although Dodson and Miller-Jones and all those guys had done the work to get New Britain where it was. I certainly was tired. Among the Texas, the regionals, the college world series, Winter Haven, New Britain, and the Eastern League play-offs, I'd thrown 298 innings. It certainly had been a successful season; all told, I'd won 26 games and struck out close to 300 batters. My professional record (9–2, 1.19, 96 hits, 108 strikeouts, 14 walks in 98 innings) was extremely satisfying, and while I needed a rest, when the Red Sox asked me to come to Boston in September for a couple of days, see Fenway, and work out, I couldn't wait.

When I got to Boston, I knew I wasn't going on the roster and be activated, but I got a tremendous thrill when I walked into the clubhouse, found that I already had a locker, and hanging in it was my number: 21. I don't know how clubhouse man Vinnie Orlando knew to give me 21. He said he'd watched me in the college world series on ESPN, so maybe that was it. But that's my family number. I didn't have it at Spring Woods, where I wore 40 (which they retired alongside former Olympic basketball gold medalist Tate Armstrong), but everywhere else it's been 21. The irony of that is that there were two other prominent Texas pitchers for the Red Sox who wore 21—Tex Hughson, who helped pitch them to the 1946 pennant, and Ray Culp, an Austin boy. I put on that number 21 in the Red Sox clubhouse and guys came up telling me to ask for another number. "Do you know who Mike Torrez is?" asked one player after another. "This is my number," I'd reply. "Don't worry. I'll take care of the jinx or whatever it is." Bob Stanley told me I was crazy, but I considered myself lucky. If the Astros had selected me, I'd never have gotten it because Terry Puhl is 21 and they wouldn't begin to think about taking it away from an established player and giving it to some rookie out of college.

The number was important to my family. My mother kept telling me that someday she expected me to strike out 21, so after the 20-strikeout game, I told her that she had it mixed up. When I covered first and took the throw from Buckner, that putout meant that I had gotten 21 outs and that's her 21. Anyway, Randy wore 21 in high school, and he and Kathy got married on the 21st. I wore 21 in high school in football, and wore it at Texas. When I got my signing bonus, I bought my mother her first diamond ring, and it turned out to have 21 diamonds in it, without any planning or forethought. In October, Debbie and I started dating. Naturally, it turned out to be on the 21st (when we went on our honeymoon to Hawaii, the airline gave us seats 21A and 21B). It was funny. We'd known each other in high school, but we each had dated other people. She dated one of my teammates, and as I found out later, he didn't much like me, and Deb didn't much like the girl I was dating. We ran into each other after the '83 season, found out that we weren't dating anyone regularly, and started going out. She's an outstanding athlete, so we began working out together. The following April, we were engaged. That was a peculiar story, too. Debbie had been going through trials for the Dallas Cowboy Cheerleaders. She'd gone through all but the final stage, and I'd already gone through spring training and had been sent to Pawtucket when she slipped and broke her elbow, which was a tough thing for her. I told the Pawtucket people that I was flying home for two days to be with her, and they said I couldn't, that she was only my girlfriend and that there was no need to leave. I was adamant. I wasn't going to miss a start, so I flew home to see her, I asked her to marry me, and I got back in time to win my next start for Pawtucket.

I went to spring training in 1984 as a nonroster invitee, and I thought I had shown enough to go north with the Red Sox. My first major league spring training surprised me because there was so little conditioning. Our workouts consisted of something like six 60-yard dashes across the outfield, and by the third week I was in worse shape than when I reported. I kept figuring there must be something else coming, so I only did a few extra sprints. Finally, I realized that that's all there was, and I started coming to the park early to stretch, stayed late afterward to get in my running, and got catcher Jeff Newman to play long toss with me. I didn't allow a run in my first start in Winter Haven, which ironically was against the Tigers. On the bus ride over, one of the guys who had played for Lakeland the previous summer told the story of my hitting the player, and I guess he told it as if I'd done it intentionally. Manager Sparky Anderson told him to shut up and not spread the story, which told me that a thrown baseball is an intimidating factor on any level.

I had a couple of starts that spring where I gave up some runs. Pirates' first baseman Jason Thompson hit a three-run homer off me in Bradenton on a curveball, but it wasn't a monster shot or anything. When Manager Ralph Houk called me into his office and told me I was going to Pawtucket, I was pretty disappointed. Later, Alan Hendricks explained to me that there was no way I'd open the season in Boston because the club wasn't going to let me get in the two full years I needed for arbitration right off the bat. Little did I know that the following August the new collective bargaining agreement would raise the requirement for going to salary arbitration from two to three full years. If I'd gone north with the Red Sox, I'd have been able to arbitrate after the 1985 season, no matter how disappointing it had been. That would have meant that I would have had arbitration after 1986 with the MVP, Cy Young, and all those good things. I can see why they sent me out. Oh well, the Yankees did the same thing to Don Mattingly.

In Pawtucket I quickly got to know people and adjust to the professional life and enjoy it. Al Nipper and I were already becoming good friends. In fact, we were part of a stunt that spring training that was one of the funniest things I've ever seen. Malpeso and I were driving back from dinner one night when this woman in a Mercedes rammed Mal's car. She didn't do much damage, but Mal had had his eyes and heart set on this car he'd seen a lot around Winter Haven. So, after calling the insurance adjuster, he got a bright idea. "If we wreck it up pretty good, I'll get more money," he said, and began thinking. The next night after the game we walked over to the cafeteria at the Winter Haven Mall as Mal finished his plan. Nip didn't want to come along. He said he needed sleep. While we were eating, the insurance guy came, examined the car, and made his estimate. Problem is, when Mal and I got back, Nip was gone. He says to this day that the insurance guy had already come. So we got into the car, drove out in the dark to some orange grove and found a light pole.

Mal had me get out of the car, he buckled himself in and began backing the car into the pole. He'd pull way up forward, slam it into reverse at ten, then twenty, miles an hour and crash it. His neck was whiplashing, and I was standing out there, laughing and yelling, "Not good enough, Mal, get this taillight." You can imagine his surprise when we found Nipper a couple of hours later. To make it worse, Malpeso ended up going to that car dealer and getting that car. He was making only $14,000, and he got taken on this fancy $12,000 Trans-Am. He brought it back to the Holiday Inn, proud as can be, and when Nipper asked him about the financing, he shrugged. He pulled out the papers, handed them to Nip, and found out he'd been screwed. He was going to pay $30,000 for a $12,000 automobile. Poor Mal. He played this last season in Italy.

I didn't have to stay long at Pawtucket. I made six starts, was 2–3 with a 1.93 ERA, got called up to the Red Sox May 11 when they were in Kansas City, and was told that I'd start on the fifteenth in Cleveland. The Sox were having some problems at the time. Dave Stapleton, Jerry Remy, and Glenn Hoffman—three-quarters of the infield—were hurt. Hurst was pitching very well, but Dennis Eckersley was struggling, Oil Can had been sent to Pawtucket on May 6, and the club was beginning a transitional period.

I have never been more nervous than that first start in Cleveland. Everyone was there. My mother had flown in from Houston with Bonnie. Randy and Kathy had driven over from Troy, Ohio, where he was coaching at the time. My grandmother came in from Detroit. Randy and I sat down and talked an hour before the game, but I don't think there was any way that I could have imagined all the things the Indians would try: steals, squeezes, hit-and-runs, double steals, stepping out. . . . I gave up a run in the first inning when Pat Tabler singled to the opposite field, stole second, and scored when Andre Thornton hit a ball through the middle. I lasted 5⅔ innings, during which time they stole six bases, there were a couple of fielding mishaps, and Mike Easler even got charged with interference at first base in a wild four-run fourth inning that put us behind 5–0. I was nervous and didn't have good command of myself or my pitches, as I walked three and got behind some hitters. But in that four-run inning, three batters reached on balls in the infield and the only ball that was hit at all hard was Tony Berna- zard's two-run double, and that was an opposite field job down the left field line. It was 5–4 when Houk took me out, and we tied it up 5–5 before losing 7–5, which meant that I had my first big league no-decision.

I got my first big league win in my next start in Minnesota, and pitched quite a bit better. I went seven innings, allowed four runs, and struck out seven before Stanley pitched two perfect innings to save the 5–4 win. I felt pretty good about it. One run came on an infield hit, stolen base, and fly ball; two others on an opposite field double and an opposite field single. In my third start, against Kansas City, I left with two out and two on in the seventh inning, with a 5–3 lead. Poor Stanley. He came in and George Brett greeted him with a triple to tie it. Then Hal McRae singled to put the Royals ahead. Center fielder Tony Armas hit a two-run homer in the bottom of the seventh to put us back in front, 7–6, but the Royals scored five runs off Stanley and John Henry Johnson in the eighth for an 11–7 win.

I learned a lesson in the days after that start. In talking to some reporter, I said that I liked to finish games, which was meant to be nothing but a generic comment. The writer then added in that I obviously liked to finish them because of the Red Sox bull pen. Stanley reads everything that's in the papers. Sometimes I think he worries too much about what's written or said, but in this in- stance he took offense and accused me of getting on the bull pen, which I wasn't. At that point in the season, we were virtually tied with the Indians for last place. The Tigers were 35–5 before that Saturday afternoon we played the Royals, and we were eighteen games out only forty-five games into the season. But that Friday they'd traded Eckersley and Brumley, who was playing for New Britain, to the Cubs for Bill Buckner, who had a tremendous impact, both offensively and defensively. Marty Barrett was establishing himself at second, Jackie Gutierrez was playing well at short, and stars such as Jim Rice and Dwight Evans—who were hitting .238 and .220—began to get hot. Oil Can got himself straightened out in Pawtucket, came back on May 30, and was 12–9 with ten com- plete games from that point on. Nip went into the rotation on June

5 and won eleven games. So with the three of us and Hurst and Bobby Ojeda, we seemed to have one of the best young rotations in baseball — with Rich Gedman as catcher, directing and helping us. From that weekend when we lost to the Royals through the end of the season, we had the second-best record in the league. The Tigers, who swept through the play-offs and World Series losing only one game, were only one game better than we were after May 27.

At this point, I was learning several lessons about the big leagues, for after all I was less than a year out of a Longhorn uniform. One of the basic changes is pitching to wooden bats. In college, if you pitch inside and jam a batter, the aluminum bat will get it out over the infield. Randy and I had talked about the difference when I signed, and right away in Winter Haven I began noticing that when I got it in with the wooden bats, I either broke them or hitters couldn't get around on the ball. I think my tendency in college was to pitch more up and down. In the big leagues, I was learning to go in and out even more than up and down, but it took a while to realize what I could do. I wasn't seeing any holes, and when I started getting hit a little, I lost my concentration and got a little overpumped. All I could think about was what the hitters could do, which is backward. It's a funny thing about some scouting reports. All they do is tell pitchers what *not* to throw hitters, but it's the defense that's the offense in baseball: the pitcher has the ball, and what the hitter does is predicated on what the pitcher does, not vice versa. But sometimes you hear, "This guy is a high fastball hitter, so don't throw him a fastball," which doesn't always make sense because it's backward. When I'm thinking about hitters hitting, sometimes all I see is them hitting instead of their holes, and that's what I did for a while that season. I was pitching defensively. I had a good outing in Milwaukee on June 2, beating the Brewers 6–3 despite giving up two homers to shortstop Robin Yount — now *there* is a great high fastball hitter — to make my record 2–0. But then I hit a little rough spot for two starts. The Brewers got thirteen hits and six runs off me in 5⅔ innings to hand me my first loss, 6–3. Then in my next outing, against the Yankees, I not only came close to getting my leg torn off when Mattingly hit me with a liner through the middle, but I gave up eight hits, a wild pitch, and six runs in 3⅔ innings. Fortunately, relievers Steve Crawford and Stanley kept us in the game, and Evans hit a three-run homer off Dave Righetti in the eighth for a 9–8 victory.

My next start was going to be on a Sunday in Toronto, and that Friday Lee Stange sat down with me for a pitching coach–pitcher chat. Stinger was good to me. (I used to also call him Skip, which he didn't like because Houk was the skipper and the Major was definitely the Boss.) "Let the ball go," he told me. "With your stuff and control, if you let it go, you'll win. It's as simple as that. If there were anything wrong with you, we'd have tried to change you —and no one has any intention of changing you. Even if you get hammered Sunday, you're not going anywhere. You'll make your next start against Toronto next weekend. You're here. Period."

Stange did make a couple of suggestions. One was that perhaps I was throwing too many strikes. The second was that I try a four-seam curveball. One good thing about both Stange and Bill Fischer as pitching coaches is that while they each offer suggestions that one can try, they don't tell you that you have to do it. They realize every pitcher is different and that some things work for some, other things work for others. The four-seam curveball helped, just as the next year getting the cross-seam fastball from Fischer really opened up my repertoire the way Seaver later told me that learning that pitch changed his whole career. That 1984 season I seemed to have a very good curveball.

That Sunday, June 17, start in Toronto got stopped after four innings by rain, but I think I started to turn a corner during that game. I really aired it out—struck out seven and allowed only one hit— and the following Friday, I beat the Blue Jays 8–1 and struck out nine. However, I still had some more lessons to learn, as I went thirty-four days before winning again. After a 3–1 loss to the Orioles, I had three subpar starts, allowing six runs in seven innings against Oakland; nine hits and four runs in 4⅓ innings against California; and finally, eight hits and four runs in 2⅔ innings in Seattle. In that game in Seattle, I faced seventeen batters; eight got hits. At that point my record was 3–4, my earned run average was 5.94, the league was hitting .326 against me, and I'd allowed ninety-seven hits in 69⅔ innings.

After that Seattle game, reporters were asking both Houk and me what I guess was a fair question: had I been rushed too fast? The name David Clyde—that magic name that I'd been hearing since I was a junior in high school—was brought out of the closet and traced to some factory job in Houston. That's when Ralph sat me down. He told me I was going to miss one start, that I should throw on the side and get my mechanics back, and then I'd go right back into the rotation. "You're a good major league pitcher; you ain't going anywhere," he repeated. Hurst sat me down and gave me a lecture about how good I was and how these things happen in the big leagues, the same lecture I had to give him a year later. Randy reminded me that I always said I'd know that I'd made it when I pitched to Reggie Jackson; I loved the way Reggie craved the pressure and performed so well, and I used to pray that he'd stay around long enough to still be there when I made it. So when I struck him out, Randy told me I could throw my glove down right there and retire. Five days later, I threw two innings in relief in Oakland, and eight days after that I started against the White Sox. That was the start of a six-game winning streak that lasted until I hurt my forearm in Cleveland on August 31.

What I worked out on the side was more mental than physical. I simply got my thinking straight, reestablished in my mind what I had to do to be successful, and regained my concentration. When I struggled, I was getting to the mound and forgetting what I was supposed to do because I'd get excited. When I started again on July 26—eleven days after Seattle—it all came back together. I got my first big league shutout that night against the White Sox, striking out eleven. I beat the White Sox in Chicago in my next start, beat the Tigers, and on August 11, got to go back to Texas with all my family and friends watching and beat the Rangers. On August 21, I had my finest game to that point, beating Kansas City 11–1, striking out fifteen without walking anyone. The next day, someone researched that I was only the fourth pitcher ever to strike out as many as fifteen without walking anyone. Then I threw a three hitter and struck out ten to beat Cleveland 4–2 and up my record to 9–4, which I guess was the clincher on my being named the American League pitcher of the month for August.

At that point, I was thinking about fourteen or fifteen wins, and when I went back out to pitch against the Indians in Cleveland on August 31, I was off on what I thought was a fifteen- to eighteen-strikeout night. Evans and Gedman had hit two-run homers, and I had just finished striking out outfielder Joe Carter in the bottom of the fourth—which gave me seven strikeouts out of eleven outs.

I was pitching to Andre Thornton when I felt this sharp pain in my forearm. It really hurt, sort of a grabbing sensation. As soon as I grabbed my arm, Houk was running at full speed out of the dugout. I tried to throw again, but it didn't feel right. I wanted to keep going, but I've always tried to be honest with my managers and coaches, and when I told Ralph it still hurt, I was in the clubhouse.

At the time, I was scared. So was Randy. Now, there's no question that all the innings I'd thrown over the last couple of years had something to do with the strain. But it turned out to be nothing more than a pull, a strained tendon in my forearm, which had nothing to do with my elbow or shoulder. In a period of a week or ten days, I was throwing all right again, nine innings on the side, and I still thought I could win twelve or thirteen games and help the team finish up strong. But Houk wouldn't let me pitch. First he told me he didn't want to take any chances with me. But then he told me that he would have let me pitch, only he was under orders from upstairs not to let me go out there again. I didn't know what was going on, but both Alan and Randy Hendricks told me that winter that again it had something to do with arbitration down the line and keeping my numbers down at the time. That was a little hard for me to understand, but all in all it had been a satisfying rookie season. I finished 9–4, the team finished strong, and we believed we and the Royals had the best young rotations in the league. One article late in the season stated that the Mets, Royals, and Red Sox had the best young pitching in baseball and would win at least two World Championships among them in the next three years. It turned out to be true in just *two* years.

All through the winter, to the Boston Baseball Writers dinner, through to spring training in 1985, I was faced with a barrage of questions about my arm. That drove me a little crazy, because there wasn't anything wrong with my arm. By November, I was fully into my program of running, lifting weights, and doing legwork. Deb and I got married — with Schiraldi, Capel, Nipper, and Oil Can all in the wedding party — in November and went to Hawaii for our honeymoon. When we got back, I went to Boston to be checked out and began throwing by Christmas. We went to Winter Haven early, and Nip, Oil Can, and I were all throwing and working out every day. I was fine, but once spring training started, I felt as if

Manager John McNamara and Fischer were babying me. I'd ask
Johnny Pesky, the assistant to the general manager, to hit me
grounders and line drives, and he backed off. I tried to play long
toss, and they didn't want me to. Then CEO Haywood Sullivan
came and told me to stop pumping weights; it seems someone had
told him that I was doing all sorts of powerlifting, which annoyed
me, because in fact all I was doing were weights exercises to maintain my shoulder and leg strength.

Nip, Can, and I had to have our contracts settled down there, too.
That turned out to be a little unpleasant just because Can got so upset. He and his agent, Dennis Coleman, were making all kinds of
threats to the club—Can walked out one day—but what bothered
Nip and me so much was that Can publicly said that he deserved to
make more money than either of us because he'd had the better season. He had pitched well. Very well. He won and completed more
games than either of us. But it didn't seem fair to bring us into the
thing in the papers. It especially hurt Nip, because he and Can had
been good friends all through their careers in Winter Haven, Bristol,
Pawtucket, and Boston. We realized that Can is excitable and gets
upset, but he and Coleman brought other players into it a couple
of times. When Can went home in spring training of 1986 to have
a physical at UMass-Worcester and some television reporter raised
a rumor of drugs, Coleman asked, "How come no one asks about
drugs when Al Nipper goes to the hospital or when Bob Stanley
doesn't perform well?" That not only hurt Nip, but set both him
and Stanley off into tirades. Coleman was lucky to escape Winter
Haven alive, and Can had to go out of his way to apologize.

By the time we left Winter Haven to open the 1985 season, we
felt good about our chances. We'd finished strong the year before,
the team in the field was strong, we had Buckner and Barrett in
the lineup from the start, and the starting pitching had come together. The one setback was Nipper ending up in the hospital with
ulcers. That was pretty scary when he started passing blood and
had the blood disorder. He was afraid for a while that it was leu-
kemia, so when he learned that it was an ulcer, in a way he was
relieved. On the other hand, we'd been down in Winter Haven early,
working out together, and he was in great shape and looking forward
to a big year, so he never really did get back in sync. He didn't join
us until April 15, and even then he was pushing himself.

The one big change at the end of spring training was putting

Ojeda in the bull pen. He'd been our top winner (12–7, 12–12) each of the last two years, but management felt that if and when Nip were healthy—and with the addition of Bruce Kison—our starting rotation was strong enough so that our need for a left-handed reliever had to be filled with Ojeda. The move made sense from the standpoint of Ojeda's being a great competitor. The question was whether Bobby, who is primarily a fastball–change-up pitcher who throws his curveball to get the feel of the change-up, could pitch out of the pen using primarily his fastball. As it turned out, he couldn't. The big thing, he said, was that he didn't have time to work himself out of trouble, which was a trademark as the Astros and Red Sox both know from their sixth games. He said he'd have some trouble and was gone. He basically had lost his change-up in the bull pen, and when they put him back in the rotation, he wasn't the same pitcher the rest of the year. So McNamara and Fischer never saw how good he was until the World Series in 1986.

I felt fine. It always takes a power pitcher time to put all the parts of his delivery together, as I found out the next spring, but I was ready when the 1985 season opened. There didn't seem to be any problems in the transition from Houk to McNamara, or—in the pitchers' case—from Stange to Fischer. Some of the pitchers, notably Mark Clear and Hurst, were somewhat hesitant accepting Fischer at first. When Bruce got off to that 2–7 start and the club tried so hard to trade him—they first tried to deal him even-up for John Tudor, then offered him to Toronto before the trading deadline for Luis Leal (who this past winter was on the Knoxville roster) —he was actually calling his old Pawtucket coach Mike Roarke in St. Louis for advice. Hurst and Fischer eventually clicked. Fish tells Bruce, "One day out of five you were one of the biggest jerks I've ever met." But Fischer got him to use his forkball and try the cross-seamer, and he's been one of the best left-handers in the game ever since.

Fischer is a great believer in the cross-seam fastball, which makes the ball take off high in the strike zone. One of baseball's oldest adages is that pitchers always have to keep the ball down. Fischer doesn't believe that. He feels that 90 or more percent of hitters are low-ball hitters. He'll tell you that it's actually a shorter distance to the plate when you pitch up and that today—with so many hitters adopting the Charlie Lau theory, standing away and diving into the ball—hitters have more trouble catching up to the ball when it's up. I used to throw the traditional with-the-seams fastball that either sank or ran, but throwing across the seams and getting that little extra jump added to my game. As the combination of the forkball and cross-seamer gave Bruce two whole new planes to go with his sinker and great curveball, so having this fastball gave me a whole new plane upstairs for hitters to think about. To chase that fastball or not to chase it as it explodes up and out of the strike zone is a tough instantaneous decision for a batter, and it allowed me to go up and down and in and out and seemed to make my strike zone larger.

We were all excited when we started the season by sweeping the Yankees three straight at home. I followed Can and Hurst and won the third game 6–4, and when Can beat the White Sox 7–2 we were 4–0 and the whole town was going crazy. Coleman was already talking to reporters about Can starting the All-Star Game after the opener, when Dave Winfield and a couple of other Yankees got into it with Can over his actions on the mound. McNamara was still thinking about bringing me along slowly and not putting pressure on me by making me the third or fourth starter—being careful— and I got off to a decent start. In my second outing, I lost 2–0 in Kansas City to a masterpiece by Danny Jackson, then went through a bit of a dry spell, losing three out of four. Right around the first of May, I felt as if I were getting it together. I beat California, lost to Oakland, then on May 17 in Cleveland threw my first shutout and had my first ten-strikeout game of the season.

I don't get much of a kick out of Cleveland jokes, for it was a cold Friday night on Lake Erie—or the ocean, as Can calls it—that I pulled the muscle in my forearm the previous August. And it was that night that I first felt something wrong in my shoulder. Again, it was cold, damp, and windy, and when I woke up the next morning I was stiff as a board. I knew I wasn't going to pitch again until Thursday in Minnesota, so because I was so stiff I took it easy with my arm the next couple of days, and after we lost Sunday to drop us to 16–19, we flew to Minnesota. I woke up there and was still stiff. The Hyatt-Regency in Minneapolis has a pool, a health club, and a basketball court, so I went upstairs and swam a little. When I got to the park, I threw on the side, and I felt terribly sluggish, as if I were really, really heavy. I started Thursday night in the Metrodome, which turned out to be a tough 4–3 game with Frank Viola. I felt that I was forcing myself, that I wasn't right. However,

I was forcing enough to be clocked at 97. I learned a lesson there, too. They were putting the radar gun readings up on the message board, and when I saw I was hitting 97, I'd rear back, force it and try to hit 98 and 99, which turned out to be a painful part of learning. My arm was heavy and I wasn't thinking, and when I got back to the hotel I felt a stinging pain that I'd never experienced before. I was taking anti-inflammatory medicine, but I knew something wasn't right. I figured it was important not to keep it to myself, to let Fischer and (trainer) Charlie Moss know how I felt and how much it worried me. I tried to distinguish between hurting and injury. There's a subtle difference. My pain tolerance has always been pretty decent. As a child, I almost lost my eye when I flipped a weight bench while working out, and walked away. I played the second half of a football game on a broken ankle, and walked away. But my shoulder is my livelihood, and I figured that if there was some tendinitis or something, I'd better find out precisely what the problem was. I had some bicep tendinitis in college, pitched through it, and went on from there.

I wasn't going to pitch that weekend in Texas, so they sent me home to Boston as a precautionary measure. For two weeks or so, I'd explain to Dr. Pappas, Rich Zawacki (the physical therapist), Charlie Moss, Fischer, and McNamara how I felt, then I'd go out to the bull pen to throw for ten or fifteen minutes and I'd get it up there at 92 or 93 miles an hour. I guess at that point I was puzzling them and had them wondering what in the world was going on in my shoulder and head. The problem was that I could go throw hard for that period of time, but I couldn't keep it up. While they were probably wondering about what makes me tick, I was asking, "Is this something new? Hasn't this ever happened before? Is this some unique disease? It hurts here and it hurts there, so what the heck is it?"

The combination of the fear, anxiety, and frustrations made for a lot of inner turmoil. I took my regular start May 27 and beat the Twins 9–2, which made my record 6–4, 3.44; and I was in a 4–1 stretch since May 7. But I wasn't getting better, only worse, and by the sixth inning I was getting by throwing only 85 mph. They told me it was bicep tendinitis, so I took some medicine and rested for five days. Then it hurt in the back of the shoulder, then down deeper in the shoulder. I tried another start or two, but it was the same problem. I kept telling people that it was getting better. I wanted to pitch, and I figured that I'd won in high school throwing in the low 80s, so I can find a way to win in the big leagues no matter how I throw. But, finally, on our second trip to California, it all caved in.

I was scheduled to start the Sunday, July 7, game at California. I started to warm up by playing long toss, as I always do. The joint was very stiff, as if I somehow needed to get it lubricated. Then, when I started my throwing, I felt an intensely sharp pain, as if someone stuck a knife in the back of my shoulder. I'd never felt anything like it before, and I kept telling myself that here I'd found a real challenge to my pain tolerance. "I can put up with it and get us to the seventh," I muttered to myself. I wasn't ready to set the ball down, for if it were simply tendinitis, it should go away with anti-inflammatory medicine and aspirin. During all this time, I didn't take any shots, thank goodness. The only thing I tried was Indocin; actually, I tried a cortisone tablet, but it upset my stomach. I kept telling Fischer I could make it into the seventh, but finally he grabbed the phone, called McNamara in the dugout, and told him that there was no way they could allow me to pitch. "Get back in the clubhouse, you're going back to Boston," he told me, and I started the long walk in from the left field bull pen to the first base dugout in Anaheim Stadium.

By the time I reached the clubhouse, about all I had on were my sliding shorts. I grabbed that heavy metal door that goes from the clubhouse to the dugout runway and tore it off its hinges. Somewhere in the runway I must have torn my jersey off, for there were buttons everywhere. I kicked off one shoe somewhere down there, then kicked the other one across the clubhouse. I fired my glove into one trash can, my pants and socks into another trash can, and picked up the chair and fired it into my locker. I finally sat down, put on my running shorts and shoes and started out the door into the big hallway that runs all around the stadium. I started to go to the stairs and go outside, then leaned against the wall and slumped to the floor. Nip could see what I was going through, came running in from the dugout, through the clubhouse, and burst into the hallway. At that point, I had tears in my eyes and I kept asking, "Why me?" He consoled and comforted me as best he could. "Roger, this isn't career threatening," he kept telling me. "They'll find what the problem is. You're just sidetracked, you're not finished." I kept mumbling and talking about pain. I don't think I made a lot of sense, but honestly, it was more frustration and confusion than fear, because I'm not afraid of pain.

Nip had to go back down to the dugout for the start of the game, so I went up the flight of stairs, walked out into the parking lot, and took off. It was a hot July afternoon in Anaheim, about 90 degrees. As I ran, I thought about playing with the broken ankle or breaking my nose three or four times or what pain tolerance really is. I ran about as hard a pace as I could, with tears in my eyes from the frustration. "*Junkballer,*" I thought. I started thinking about coming up with a trick pitch and coming back as a trick 'em pitcher. Power pitchers don't last forever. I figured maybe I'd just have to start my makeover early. "*Hitter,*" I thought. I was a pretty good hitter in high school. If I couldn't pitch, I'd go back to A ball and try to make it as a first baseman.

After forty-five minutes I remember coming to the end of a long street and lying down in the grass of some business. I lay there in the sun, thinking about what I was going to do, and how unraveling it feels when you go from striving for greatness to striving to hold on in less than two months. Finally, I got up and ran back to the ballpark before the game was over, showered, and got ready to take a cab to Los Angeles International Airport for the flight back to Boston to be reexamined. The first day I got home, someone wrote a column suggesting that there wasn't anything legitimately wrong with me, that I was a head case. *That* angered me. I was so mad I could have killed the guy, and I told a couple of reporters two weeks later that he might be a nice guy and a good writer and all that, but if he came near me I might just explode and go after him, which I didn't want to do. Things were building in me that badly. I kept asking how I could throw four, five, or six good innings, then have nothing, and I told Dr. Pappas that we had to try something else because whatever we were doing wasn't working. It was frustrating for him and Rich Zawacki, too, because they'd go with me to the bull pen and I'd throw in the 90s. But that was still the bull pen, where I wouldn't push that final 2 or 3 percent past the threshold as I would when in game competition.

I rested and tried again. First I pitched in Cooperstown on August 5 in the exhibition against the Astros. I felt good, and I threw hard, and the five-inning stint was encouraging. That day I happened to start an important part of my rehabilitation, although I was almost a month before an operation. I had heard that Nolan Ryan had a poster out with a series of shoulder exercises, so I talked to him and he showed me what he does in his program to keep his shoulder strong. That man astounds me. He's nearly forty years old and can still throw in the high 90s, a testament to conditioning, strong legs, and dedication. I made my regular start the following Saturday in Kansas City, went five pretty good innings, and got the win. It was a win, but I still didn't feel right. When I started to feel my shoulder deadening and tiring in the fourth inning, I went up into the clubhouse and played catch with Nip to keep it lubricated and loose.

Then, on August 11, came the end. It was one of those nationally televised Sunday games between the Yankees and Red Sox. I was facing Ron Guidry, which made it big, but when I started warming up, I could tell I wasn't right. I yelled at Fischer. He kept asking me how I felt . . . how I felt, how I felt . . . how I felt. And I hollered, "Quit asking me how I feel—touch me, why don't you?" Some New York fan yelled at me from the bleachers behind the bull pen, and I fired a ball against the screen in his direction. After a couple of more pitches, I said I was ready, that it was a hot day. What I really was thinking was that I didn't want to leave it in the bull pen. This time I was going up to the clubhouse and was going to throw to Nip between every inning because I knew I couldn't let the shoulder idle. I threw the ball well—at least 88 miles per hour—for three innings. I struck out three of the first eight batters. Then I went out for the fourth and it wasn't the same. Marc Sullivan was catching me that day, and the next spring he told me that when I delivered the first three pitches with three different motions at three different locations at three different speeds, home plate umpire Ken Kaiser leaned over his shoulder and said, "What the heck is going on with that guy?" The Yankees got a run that inning, but I got out, went up to the clubhouse, and kept throwing. When I walked Butch Wynegar, their catcher, in the fifth, I unconsciously started shrugging my shoulder. Out came McNamara. "I'm just tiring, I'm not having any pain," I insisted. "If I stay closed in my delivery, I'll be all right."

I got the side out in order, and after the inning Dr. Pappas, Zawacki, Moss, and McNamara confronted me in the runway as I started up to the clubhouse to keep throwing. "I won't mess this thing up for you," I told Mac, and he shot back, "I'm not worried about this stupid game, I'm worried about you and your career."

Mac apparently told Sullivan to let him know if he detected any-thing odd in my delivery, and before I could finish my eight warm-up tosses, Marc stepped out from behind the plate and motioned for McNamara. "He's gritting his teeth on warm-up pitches," Sulli-van told the manager. "He's falling off the mound, his arm is all cockeyed." McNamara asked me for the ball and signaled for Steve Crawford.

At that point, they were still saying that my problem was tendini-tis and that I was suffering from shoulder fatigue. I tried throwing between starts again, couldn't keep it up, and finally they put me back on the disabled list. If the Red Sox had been in the pennant race at that point, I'd have continued to try and pitch. But we were still under .500 and out of it, and frankly, things weren't too good. It was a funny club at that point. It was a clubhouse of great guys, but somehow the Red Sox had all been individuals for so long that everyone went his way, as whoever it was said years ago when he claimed the Red Sox are the only team that gets off a plane and goes in twenty-five separate cabs, twenty-four with the owners stick-ing to the smaller roster to save a few pennies. Finally, in late Au-gust, it was decided that I had to have some sort of exploratory arthroscopic surgery. Both Alan Hendricks and my brother Randy insisted that I get a second opinion, not because we questioned Dr. Pappas, but because this was such an important matter. Alan talked to a bunch of people and decided that the best man for me to see was Dr. James Andrews in Columbus, Georgia. I was upset, sure. I'd said that if I ended up having surgery I was going to be mad at a lot of people who couldn't identify the problem and let me pitch those games in August, but that was sort of irrational.

Dr. Andrews examined me, identified the problem, and we decid-ed right there to let him do the surgery in consultation with Dr. Pappas. Again, I had nothing against Dr. Pappas, but he rarely per-forms arthroscopic surgery, and Dr. Andrews is one of the men who revolutionized this business. A small piece of cartilage had broken off. It became inflamed and was pinching the joint when I rotated to throw. It rubbed and rubbed and rubbed, and caused daggerlike pain. Dr. Andrews explained that when I was a freshman at San Jacinto and still growing, I was building up to 91 miles an hour, and I was building everything else up without building up the four muscles in my shoulder and throwing three hundred innings a year until finally my shoulder just said "forget it." He explained that everyone gets a buildup of cartilage, and that this piece could have been the result of a hit in high school football. Randy, my mother, Deb, Alan, and I talked it over with him, and the operation was scheduled for the next morning. "This is minor surgery," Dr. Andrews told me. "How you recover depends entirely on how religiously you work at the rehabilitation."

The operation was so simple that it took only twenty minutes, and I was able to watch on the monitor. The piece of cartilage wasn't big at all. He just zipped in with a little Pac-Man, scooped it out, vacuumed around the rotator area, and when he was done he replayed the tape and explained it all to us. He had a skeleton there and showed me what exercises I should do. "What makes this so minor is that you're already so strong," he told me. What I'd done is begin my rehab three weeks before the operation, which is why I was able to be the first patient Dr. Andrews has ever had that worked out the day after the operation. (That night, I went over to the ballpark in Columbus to see Noble, just for a reminder of what it's like in the minors. Someone once said that it's tougher the second time around in the minors, after you've been in the big leagues. Now I know it's true.) I'd been on a program for three weeks, using different facets of the exercises suggested by Ryan, Dr. Pappas, and Dr. Frank Jobe, whose book I read while I was sitting out. If I had known about the muscles in my shoulder and understood both what they do and what I have to do to maintain them, I never would have had the breakdown in the first place. I realized that might-have-beens weren't going to get me pitching again, so I began the program. I was doing the exercises twice a day. I started with no weights, then progressed to 1½ pounds on the wrist, then to 2 and 2½; when I got to 3 by the end of September, I was ready to climb up to 5.

I do all different exercises exclusively for the rotator cuff area today, and don't worry about weight. If you do them correctly with 3 pounds, not only are they sufficient, but they'll wear you out. Now that I'm healthy, I do only 3 and 5 pounds. I know guys who try to go to 7½ pounds, and they blow themselves out. The important thing is doing them correctly. At the end of this past season, Coach Maiorana asked me to talk to the Spring Woods players about these exercises. Then I went with him to address six hundred Texas high school coaches in Waco on the same subject. They cover every part of the shoulder as well as the wrist and elbow, too. I showed Buckner and our batting coach, Walter Hriniak, who had elbow operations, my elbow exercises, and they think they've helped them. There's something called the super seven for your elbow joint and it really works. During my rehab, I was running every day and doing weights squats for my legs, to keep the rest of my body in shape.

By the first of November, I was ready to start throwing, so I began in the backyard with Deb, fifteen minutes at a time. At first she was throwing the ball back to me harder than I was getting it to her. Then I began getting stronger, so after fifteen minutes I'd stop, throw a football, then throw ten minutes of the baseball again. Right around Thanksgiving, I went up to Angelina Junior College with Deb's brother Craig, who was starting there as a freshman. I wasn't supposed to be getting on any mound, but I had the itch so badly that I went out in an intrasquad game and threw an inning for each side. I wasn't getting it up there much harder than 82 mph, but it felt good to be on a mound, pitching, and I knew I was on schedule because not only didn't I feel any pain, but I felt fluid and natural again. Not only that, but I struck out Craig, which was good for family matters. When he stepped in, he was pointing the bat at me, smiling.

I didn't tell anyone about my pitching experience, but when I went back to Worcester in December to be checked out by Rich and Dr. Pappas, they knew I was ready. I tested out strong on the cybex machine, actually stronger than I would the next December. I kept doing my running and exercises and in early January went over to Spring Woods to start throwing; by that time, I was throwing too hard for Deb—no matter how good an athlete she is—and needed a high school receiver. I was playing long toss and throwing, and while my arm felt heavy, I realized that every year when you start throwing, the shoulder feels heavy, the elbow aches, and your entire body feels sluggish. What I knew I couldn't do was rush things—and anyway, Dr. Andrews and Dr. Pappas had told me that that's exactly how I'd feel. They told me that I'd wonder if I were cuckoo, that some days I'd feel like I was throwing 110, others I'd feel as if I were throwing the shot put. In January, I started spinning breaking balls, and when I got to Winter Haven in early February, I felt I was on schedule as long as I didn't try to rush things. Nip, Calvin, Wes Gardner, and I were down there working out, and the first day Gardner really aired it out. He was throwing nasty gas on a windy, cool day with no sweatshirt, and that was the beginning of his problems. He tried to throw the next day, it began hurting, he kept having problems all spring, and he ended up pitching one inning and having a similar operation to mine.

Spring training in 1986 began normally, and I felt as if I were making progress. I was working on my forkball, and one day when I was throwing batting practice the ball was dropping so much that Rice was playfully hollering at me. Geddy thanked Rice for fouling one off because he said he might have saved his life. But it didn't cruise along smoothly. My first start was in Lakeland against the Tigers, and I felt as if I had every set of eyes in the world focused in on me, evaluating not only every pitch but every move I made. All I was thinking about was working the arm out and trying to make some good pitches, and what happened was that everything the Tigers hit found a hole. I gave up five hits and four runs in the first inning; then I stopped being so nervous. I was throwing around 87, and probably could have thrown 7 or 8 miles an hour faster, and had one-two-three second and final innings. At one point, I got a little ticked off at being hit around and wanted to start firing the ball through Gedman, but he came out, calmed me down, and told me to stick to my program. Talk about a man who knows me! Then came the hard part, which was dealing with the media questions about how I felt. I'm a person who has very high expectations, and so what someone else thinks doesn't really concern me, and I just wanted to get all the spring training work in before trying to judge how far back I'd come. I answered what I could, rode back to Winter Haven, ran a few miles, did my shoulder exercises for about an hour, and went home.

I didn't have much more success in my next outing against the Tigers, and my third time out, against Minnesota, I gave up seven runs in three innings against the Twins. I wasn't throwing that *badly*, but I was wild; my delivery was inconsistent, I walked a few guys, threw some mediocre fastballs, and gave up a grand slam to Roy Smalley—all of which meant that I'd allowed fourteen runs in eight innings over three outings. When I finished my running, I explained to writers that I had very little to say, which upset them. I understand why they had to ask me questions, but it was getting repetitious, and I felt as if I were making progress. When I got to the clubhouse, Nip and Fischer showed me the chart with the radar gun readings. I had eight or ten pitches in the 90s, a couple as high

as 93, and while I also had eight or ten fastballs in the 82–83 range,
I then knew I could get it up there again. "You're pitching backward,"
Fish told me, sternly. "You're not giving yourself credit. You're fooling around with all that slop. Go out there and let it go. You've
got your fastball back, so don't worry. You're a fastball pitcher." As
I was leaving the park, I was talking to someone about power pitchers. "Rich Gossage used to say that power pitchers take longer than
other pitchers because there are so many intricate components to
the delivery," he told me. "It takes time to build up your arm and
have your body and motion in perfect sync. If you're up into the
90s now, you're going to be OK. But you may not have it down until
the season opens. Remember, you didn't put it together until May
last year."

I went home and talked to Debbie about it and realized that that's
true. I thought back to Texas and the previous seasons, and I remembered that it took time. I thought about how I usually know when
I've thrown the hardest pitches, for they usually come when I'm
relaxed, stay back, and everything comes together naturally. Fischer
was right. I knew I had to build up my arm with fastballs and stop
worrying about the other pitches. In my next outing, in Sarasota
against the White Sox, I gave up a few runs again, and this time
I was curt with the media. "I have nothing to say at this time,"
I told them, and I know some of them thought I not only was being
arrogant but developing into a head case. Yet I had thrown the ball
well that day. I was convinced I was almost there, and in my second-
to-last outing, against the Expos on March 31, I went six innings,
gave up two earned runs, struck out four, and was even closer.

This was an odd spring training. There was a lot of negativity
around. The team had been a big disappointment the year before.
Rice was coming off a knee operation and had to take it easy. Tony
Armas was hurt and had to take it easy. Oil Can got sick, was down
to 133 pounds, had to fly home to Worcester, and people were speculating all sorts of things about him. They traded Ojeda to the Mets
for Calvin and Gardner, and both of them came down with sore
arms. I was developing a pretty good feeling because I believed that
the starting pitching was going to be a lot better than anyone realized. Hurst, Nipper, Boyd, and I all felt the same way, and in the
first week—before the regulars reported—the four of us stayed
around after others had left, did some extra running, and then sat
down in the outfield and talked. We discussed rivalries, and how

we shouldn't be pulling against one another but competing to outdo; if I pitched well, Hurst should want to top me, and if he succeeded, Can should want to follow and outdo him. We knew that we were a big key to this team. We talked a little about how pitchers were always blamed for whatever happened to the Red Sox and how they'd have to depend on us. When we were done talking, we held hands in a circle and pledged to make it our year, no matter what people were saying all around us.

So I tried to shut out all the negativity, feeling that Hurst, Boyd, Nipper, and I could erase it all if we pitched well. We knew what pitching meant to a good team. The American League East is the toughest division in baseball, and only three times have teams won it without having the best staff earned run average in the division (and two of the three that didn't had the second best ERA in the division). My last preparation for the regular season was the second-to-last game, in Kissimmee against the Astros, and it all came back. I was up around 95, struck out nine in seven innings, and when it was over, I was ready to talk. I had made up my mind that this was the day I was going to let it fly and air it out and hold nothing back, that when I got to two strikes I was going to try to throw it by people. When I did it, I realized that throwing it *by* someone was a big mental hurdle that I had to clear. Afterward, I was ready to say "I'm back," but everyone was getting ready for the trip north the next day, no one was watching, and no one cared about listening. But my two brothers were both there, and they knew.

We flew to Detroit for the opening three games, and I was going to start the fourth game in Chicago on Friday night. We flew to Chicago after the Thursday game in Detroit, and on the flight I thought about the cold and how I'd prefer 102-degree heat, but that I was no longer worried about that final 3 percent of airing it out. I knew I was getting stronger all the time, but I thought about how good I'd be again. I knew I could pitch in the big leagues again. How effectively, I still didn't know, and wouldn't until I could judge myself over the long season. But I felt good. I felt especially good about the ball club. I knew we were going to be a lot better than our fifth-place predictions, and I knew I was going to be able to contribute.

·4·
THE NIGHT OF
THE TWENTY K'S

"Anyone who had been around the Red Sox over the years knew that pitchers were considered second-class citizens. It was always the pitchers' fault that the Red Sox lost. Hitters had the stats, and even if we lost on some shoddy fielding, it was the pitchers who gave up too many runs. Of course we felt it. I was sensitive to it, Ojeda was, so was Tudor; we were referred to as 'Plague, Pestilence and Death' one time in the paper. That all changed this April, and it changed because of Roger. We'd never had a pitching presence in the clubhouse in my years with this team, but he just exudes respect. His comeback made everyone start thinking that we had a chance to win. Then the night that he struck out twenty, everyone was thinking, 'Hey, we've got a weapon that no one else has,' and that night everyone in a Red Sox uniform was convinced that we were going to win the pennant. There are impact players on the field, and there are impact players off the field. Roger Clemens is one of the rare people who is an impact player on and off the field."
—Bruce Hurst

WHEN I WENT out to warm up in Chicago that night of April 11, I could feel that the eyes of the manager and coaches were definitely on me. Fischer didn't say much of anything. I honestly wasn't nervous. I was more concerned with the White Sox and the game, and once I began warming up and my arm felt fine, I was normal. I'd talked to my brother Randy that afternoon. He is my advance scout. Now, I read the papers and check the box scores of my next opponent for the four or five days between starts, but Randy has it checked out all the way in advance. By midsummer, we had finally gotten him a satellite dish, so he could watch everyone. But until then, he'd do a lot of different things: tape games off cable, listen to games either on his radio or by calling the private number of the station and listening that way, or he'd call someone and have them put the phone next to the TV or radio. On nights when I'd pitch and my in-laws were watching on the dish in their house in Katy, Randy would call up and have them put the phone next to the upstairs TV so he could listen to my game while he watched whatever game he felt he should be watching. It's amazing what he picks up. Before this game in Chicago that April, I was curious to know if Ron Kittle had made any adjustments so that he could catch up to the high fastball. He hadn't. Randy had noticed that Carlton Fisk had made a change, though. In '85, he'd pull everything. No matter how good a fastball I ran in on him, he'd pull it, usually foul. But Randy saw that he'd changed and was now going the other way, so I'd have to adjust accordingly.

Randy picks up a ton over the season; he'd be a great addition to some organization.He could judge talent better than a lot of the scouts in the big leagues that do it for us. I know he'd be an excellent advance scout. When he gives me a call, he'll tell me what he thinks I can and cannot do to people. Just like the first time I faced Reggie. He knew I was all keyed up to face him and didn't want me to get carried away. I struck him out the first three times, but the fourth time he came up, I had a 5–2 lead and a runner on first, and he was in a position to make it a one-run game. I tried to punch him out again, but he turned up the dial and hit the ball out of the ballpark, making it 5–4. The first words out of Randy's mouth the next day were, "I told you." I argued that I got him three times, but Randy reminded me that they were all with no one on, and Reggie wasn't thinking the same way. I really can't listen to how Hurst throws someone, because I'm completely different. I'm completely different from Oil Can or Nipper, too, who throw a lot of different pitches. Randy's very good at knowing me and how *I* have to approach individual hitters as opposed to the scouting reports that we get, which are more general.

As soon as I got started in the bottom of the first on April 11 in Chicago, I knew there was nothing there bothering me in the shoulder, and the ball was running in and out. In a sense, the injury helped me, because I picked up a few things trying to learn to pitch while throwing the ball in the 80s. I learned ways to get balls in on hitters' hands. I started learning I could throw pitches a little off the plate and occasionally get them called strikes. If Gedman set up just a little out of the strike zone and I hit his glove, they often got called strikes; and Geddy is very good at shifting his glove, framing pitches and stealing a few strikes for his pitchers. Sometimes I had the tendency to make too good pitches, and I learned that it doesn't hurt to miss a little bit.

Anyway, it all felt pretty natural that night against the White Sox. Barrett hit a two-run triple in the third for a 4–1 lead, and I got within an out of a complete game before turning the 7–2 victory over to Sambito. I only struck out one, but I was throwing hard—not as hard as I knew I could or would throw—but hard enough. I still wasn't fine-tuned yet, but batters weren't getting good hacks at my high fastball either, which was an important sign.

Afterward, that whole weekend I had a lot of stiffness in my shoulder. It was in the back of the shoulder, where the injury had been, but it was just a series of knots that seemed normal and didn't scare me. I had been told to expect it, so I had to work it out by running, using the whirlpool, doing some weight work and some long tossing.

I still wasn't what I considered to be fine-tuned in my next start, April 17 against the Royals in Fenway, and I still was hesitant to really yank down hard on my curveball. Steve Balboni homered off me in the seventh to tie it at 2–2, but when Dick Howser took Mark Gubicza out, Steve Farr walked Rice to load the bases, Baylor hit a tremendous grand slam, and I finished off the complete game victory, 6–2. At that point, I still had a little stiffness, but I wasn't worried. My confidence was soaring because I was getting hitters out; I even struck out seven Royals, and I wasn't throwing that well.

It was in my third start, against the Tigers in Fenway, that things completely came together, although I left with two outs in the seventh and allowed three runs. For my third straight start, Baylor homered. We got five runs off Jack Morris early, and my delivery meshed. I let go on my curveball. My fastball was running up and out of the strike zone, and they couldn't seem to stop chasing it; I struck out ten. The next two days, I felt better than I had all spring. At that point, I felt we were about to take off.

There was a definite sense in the clubhouse that there was something going on. When we had gotten back from Chicago, we were only 3–3, but Evans had told someone, "You're going to be sorry you're not around all the time this season because we're going to win." The atmosphere in the clubhouse was completely different from what it had been either of the first two years I was there. Baylor had a big part in it. The day he arrived from the Yankees, we could all tell what an exceptional man he was. I remember Hursty jumping up and down with excitement. "One less guy I can't get out," he said. "And a great man, as well." Baylor came in and spoke in "we's." He's a big ole Texan, so that's a step in the right direction. No one in any way was taking any shot at Mike Easler, for he's a fine, fine man, but Don Baylor is almost a superman. He relates to everyone, and he speaks his mind to everyone. When the season was over and Wes Gardner, Sellers, Schiraldi, and I had to fly in to Worcester for checkups, everyone was talking about going to Baylor's house to see him. He took a lot of pressure off Rice. When Yastrzemski left and Jim was made captain, he was put in a spotlight I guess he didn't completely enjoy because he's essentially a very shy person. Baylor came over and it lightened everything for Rice. Baylor's Kangaroo Court also accomplished several things: it made us all think about little things like overthrown cutoff men, it kept our attention on the details that win games, and it gave us all a chance to laugh at ourselves and one another. There were hitters who'd come back to the bench angry as could be if they failed to move runners over, because they knew they'd get brought up in court.

Besides Baylor, I think that there were a lot of individuals in that clubhouse who were sick and tired of hearing that the Red Sox were losers. Barrett had taken some heat in the media, and he came to spring training in the best condition of his life after a winter of grueling work. Rice had been frustrated because he'd been knocked in '85 and couldn't do anything about it because of his bad knee. They all kept their mouths closed and went about their work, determined to show the writers and the fans that we had a good team if we were healthy. I felt the same way. I didn't want to stand there after I pitched and predict I'd make a successful comeback; I wanted to do it, which is why I'd walk away, go down to the AAA field and run off my frustrations. In the past, there'd been too much talk about money, and how this guy was making this or that and what he was or wasn't doing. That all seemed to get put aside by almost everyone, just to go out and prove that we could be winners.

And we pitchers had a lot to prove, which we knew and we accepted as a group that day we sat around in Winter Haven. I think that when the hitters got off to a slow start in the first month but we were still winning, and Evans, Rice, and Baylor kept saying, "Our pitching is carrying us now, and when we start hitting our pitching is good enough to win the pennant," it pulled everyone together. *Proving* something is strong motivation to an athlete. I know that when someone's said that I couldn't do something—the Twins' scout, college scouts, whoever—it pushed me. When we came out of spring training, the best we were picked was fifth, a lot of the media was making fun of us, and we felt as a team that we had something to *prove*. When we started winning in April, it pulled us closer together.

When I woke up that morning of April 29, I had a bad temple headache that stayed with me all day. I was really antsy, jittery. I was supposed to have started two days earlier in Kansas City, but it rained, so I threw in the bull pen so I wouldn't be too sluggish for the game against Seattle on the 29th. I talked to Deb about how poorly (0–2, 9.58) I'd pitched against the Mariners over my career, although I'd never faced them in Fenway. I knew that they're basically a good fastball-hitting team, but that they had also been striking out a lot (166 times in the previous nineteen games). I thought about facing Mike Moore, so I knew it would be a tough game because he's another hard thrower and one of the best pitchers in the league. I was also antsy because I was so anxious to make this such a strong start to the season. When I was en route to Chicago, I was thinking that I know I can still pitch in the big leagues, the question is how effectively. After three games, especially the way I threw the ball against the Tigers, I wanted to get out there, pitch, and get some wins because my confidence had been fully restored.

One of my biggest concerns as I warmed up was that I'd be too strong. I concentrated on trying to get the ball down, because with six days between starts I figured I'd have a lot of problems keeping the ball down in the strike zone and I didn't want to get behind too many hitters, especially good fastball hitters. I felt really strong the first two innings, really too strong. It was also a little cold, so they let me blow on my hands, but I knew from the beginning that I was up in the 90s.

First Inning: Spike Owen, Phil Bradley, and Ken Phelps struck out. Three K's. I went to 3 and 2 on all three of them. Spike can be tough for me. He's a good hitter and is just going to make contact. And he's hit me before in college, so I tried to just go after him. I got ahead, so I could try to make them run upstairs, but he fouled off a couple of pitches. In this game I was able to go in and out well, and when I get to two strikes, I figure that hard fastball down and away is my best pitch. I had the feeling that I was able to hit Geddy's glove no matter where he put it. Spike's got a good eye, but if you get ahead of him you can get him to chase the ball up. He's got better pop right-handed, but he makes better contact left-handed and it was a pretty good fastball team. He finally chased the ball.

Second Inning: Gorman Thomas lined to left. Jim Presley, Ivan Calderon struck out. Five K's. I basically threw cross-seamers and with-seamers all night. I think I threw only twenty breaking balls all night, and got fourteen of the strikeouts on the two fastballs. I had six 3-and-2 counts in the first four innings, then never went to three balls again, but my control early wasn't so bad. I got Calderon on a cross-seamer that sailed on the outside corner. It's funny. When I watched the film of the game, I could see Deb right up there behind home plate throwing her arms up in the air on every strikeout. Someday Koby will watch that tape, and we'll tell him he was there.

Third Inning: Danny Tartabull flied out. David Henderson struck out. Steve Yeager flied to center. Six K's. Henderson says he's hitting .400 off me, but no matter whom we face, he says he's hitting .400; then when I look at his average, it's closer to .200. He's had some hits off me, and he had some big homers off our staff, but he's got a big, loose swing and I have to go right after him hard. That's why I was so surprised that in the ninth inning of the fifth game of the play-offs Donnie Moore threw two fastballs by him, then threw him the forkball that he hit out.

I didn't know anything about Yeager, so I tried to be a little careful, and he hit it. I could tell it was going to be a tight game by the third inning, with the way Moore was throwing. It was cold for the hitters, two power pitchers going at each other despite the wind blowing out pretty hard. I really had the cross-seamer, and while it starts at the waist and rises up out of the strike zone, it's tough to lay off.

Fourth Inning: Owen singled to right. Bradley, Phelps, Thomas struck out in order. Nine K's. I had Spike 0 and 2, pulled down hard on a curveball, and he got a hit. That was one of my best curveballs of the year right there. Geddy was going down in the dirt. I thought, "Are you going to tell me he could hit that?" Spike just dropped down and gave it a little short, defensive swing, but I'll give him a lot of credit for staying with it. He got to first base and was laughing. I shook my head at him. I yelled, "You've got to be kidding me," and he broke out laughing again. He knew it.

With two outs and the 3–2 count on Thomas, he hit the little foul ball that kicked off Baylor's glove. Don never did look as if he had the thing under control, and he knocked it down like a goaltender making a save. Debbie Boggs turned to Deb and said, "Good, now he can strike him out." It didn't bother me. Spike was running on the play and went by the mound on his trip back to first. "What are you doing throwing at me?" he asked.

"You cost me $25 in our Kangaroo Court for that 0–2 base hit," I hollered back.

"You deserve to be fined $25 for throwing me an 0–2 curveball."

We laughed, and I got Gorman on a called third strike. Afterward, Baylor told me he dropped it on purpose.

I talked to my former UT teammate Capel, who was pitching AA in Pittsfield, the next night and related that Spike hits me pretty well. I tried to get in on him in the first inning, but the pitch was a little too far in and almost hit him. I didn't mean to come up. It was a with-the-seamer that ran in. I throw that a lot to lefthanders, but sometimes it runs back over the plate, and I get in trouble on the inside. That's what Gene Petralli hit when he hit the homer off me in Texas on national TV and kept me from winning my twentieth. It's not always easy for Gedman when I throw those two different fastballs. Sometimes I have to let him know because otherwise he can be handcuffed. I hate when it happens, but over the course of a game I'll pound on his thumb a lot. It's up to me which I'm going to throw. If he gives a sign and target for a fastball away or I shake until I get a fastball away to a righthanded batter, he knows it's usually going to be a cross-seamer because if I'm going to get it out there, I want it way out there. I don't want to run back over. That was the mistake I made to Gorman Thomas on the home run in the seventh. I had gripped it as a cross-seamer in my glove before I started my windup and changed it.

Fifth Inning: Presley, Calderon, Tartabull struck out in order.

Twelve K's. Gedman was calling as good a game as could have been called. When I had the fifteen-strikeout, no-walk game against Kansas City in '84, Jeff Newman was catching and liked to set up in the middle and not move in and out. We had it out, because I like to move around, and Gedman instinctively knows what I'm thinking.

Geddy has an extraordinary drive to be the best. I've always had good relationships with my catchers because they have such a bearing on a pitcher's success, and he's the best I've ever thrown to. He's a master at pumping my confidence, always positive and insightful. He knows what to say when he comes to the mound, and he also knows how to work around my fastball, which is my bread-and-butter pitch. I may talk about wanting to throw breaking balls, but he's got the knack of knowing when to say, "Don't get carried away with that stuff." He also knows when I'm sluggish and won't tell anyone. Sometimes, when I've got the real good fastball, he won't even give me signals; he'll just motion with his hand as if to say, "let's get it on," which is great for my psyche. He's honest about whether I've lost a little, but hey, he's honest about everything. He works and works and works on his hitting every day with Hriniak, but he's just about our most valuable player because of his knowledge of opposing hitters, his ability to handle a young pitching staff, and his defense. He's done wonders for me and my career, and I know all the other pitchers feel the same way. I don't think he's ever gotten his due credit for bringing a young starting staff along so fast. He's so quick with his release that all the pitchers have to do is get him the ball and he'll throw the guy out. He was unbelievable in the play-offs. He was so intense that he chipped three teeth grinding them while trying to sleep at night.

I guess he didn't get too much credit for anything in his first few years, and never said a thing about it. If I throw a pitch and it gets hit, he always takes the blame for calling it, even though I'm the one who threw it. I'll never forget one time last season when Lou Gorman came down into the clubhouse after a game and asked Geddy why he called for a certain pitch that got hit and cost us a win. Rich tried to be restrained, but finally he yelled, "Get out of my face, Lou."

The one thing that most of us don't understand is why Geddy hasn't gotten as much respect from the front office as he has from the players, for whom he's a leader. Some people think that some of it comes from his being so close to Hriniak, and there are a lot of people whom we hear second-guess Walter's approach. Without Geddy, though, we'd be in big, big trouble. This is no knock against anyone else, but when the other team has a left-hander starting and I'm pitching, the first thing that goes through my mind is, "Is Geddy catching?" I seldom ever shake him off more than four or five times in a game.

Striking Presley out there was especially satisfying in a close game. I think I worried more about him than anyone in the lineup, and probably did my best pitching to him because I'd thought so much about him. I didn't notice something with Tartabull until I watched the tape with Gedman. When I threw a first-pitch strike to him, he stepped out of the box and mumbled to himself, "OK, throw that again and I'll get you." Geddy noticed it though, and had me pour two more right by him.

Sixth Inning: Henderson, Yeager struck out (tying the American League record of eight consecutive strikeouts; Tom Seaver struck out ten in succession for the Mets). Owen lined to center. Fourteen K's. I got Henderson with the best sinker I threw all night, and Gedman framed the glove right around the corner and pulled it in to make sure I got the strike. I'll admit that at that point I started thinking about the strikeouts, but I was also thinking about outs, because it was still a scoreless game. I told Gedman between innings that I noticed that a few Mariners were hitching and starting their swings before I let go of the ball, so I wanted to throw a couple of breaking balls to keep them honest. I threw one 2 and 2 to Yeager, and he just took it, tipped his cap, and walked back to the dugout.

I didn't know that I'd tied a record there for consecutive strikeouts, but I knew I was on a roll and I kind of wanted to strike everyone out one time around the order. At that point, I didn't even see who was at the plate. Zoning everything out is important, and I did it that night. I didn't see anything, as opposed to the first game of the play-offs when I saw everything—the fans, the dugout, the scoreboard. I'll be honest and admit that at the end of this inning I noticed how large the crowd seemed to be getting. I think we set a record that night for most tickets sold after the sixth inning.

I missed getting them one time around the order because of Spike. It was my own fault. He'll chase the ball up, but only if he's behind in the count. I pitched him backward and tried to get him to chase it early in the count, got behind, and had to come in. He hit that ball hard, but Steve Lyons tracked it down near the warning track.

Seventh Inning: Bradley and Phelps struck out. Thomas homered into the net. Presley grounded to first. Sixteen K's. By this time, they were saying nothing in the dugout. When I'd get through and go into the runway heading up to the clubhouse to stay warm by the dryer or go in to the trainer's room, I could hear a few guys talking.

After I struck Bradley out again, I started off the mound toward the dugout, pointing to my shoes. Boggs didn't see me point to my shoes, came running over, and asked me if I was all right. He thought I'd popped my shoulder out or something, and when I said, "I need a tongue depressor to clean my spikes," he breathed a big sigh of relief.

McNamara nearly had a heart attack. He said later that he looked up, saw me heading his way, and thought about Cleveland and 1984. He was either looking down at the lineup card after the strikeout or he was gardening. (He's got this little spot in the corner where he housecleans, so we're always messing with him and throwing dirt on the steps to keep him working.) Anyway, Mac jumped over all three steps and raced out to me. I just said, "I need to clean my shoes."

I made a bad pitch that Gorman hit into the net. I should have thrown a cross-seamer, but I didn't, it was out in the middle and slightly away and stayed right there. I needed to start it out farther, too, and I was really angry. He knew a fastball was coming. The only thing I thought after I fired my glove into the dugout, went into the clubhouse, kicked my chair over, and yelled a few things was, "We had to score one run to win, anyway." The next day, Gorman asked me to autograph a ball, so I wrote, "This Time You Got Me." Gorman Thomas may retire, but he's one of the toughest and most popular players around. Everyone loves the guy.

"I can always show my kid that I was part of something that hadn't happened before and might not happen again," Gorman said. "Not only twenty strikeouts, but twenty strikeouts and no walks. That's the amazing part."

At least I covered first on Presley's grounder to Baylor, which gave me a putout and my twenty-first out. As I mentioned earlier, my mother wanted that number 21 in there somewhere. She and my sister had gone to West Houston Bowling, where they have a satellite dish, to watch the game. After the first three innings, all of a sudden some guy who worked there walked in, switched it to the Rockets game, and told them if they wanted to watch base-ball, they'd have to go somewhere else. Needless to say, none of us has been back.

Eighth Inning: Calderon struck out. Tartabull singled to right. Henderson struck out. Al Cowens pinch-hit for Yeager and flied to right. Eighteen K's. There were two outs when Evans hit a homer for the 3–1 lead, so I'd already come back down from the clubhouse and was sitting on the bench. When he hit the ball, I was the only one who didn't jump up immediately. I sat there and peeked through everybody, and once it was halfway there, I knew it was gone. Nip and I jumped up and hit the buttons of our caps on the roof of the dugout so hard that paint came off, and when Dwight got back to the dugout, I tackled him. He said he felt like I was trying to burp him.

That meant so much. I'd be the first one to admit that if I'd had a seven-run lead in the third inning, there wouldn't have been any strikeout record. There'd have been a lot more contact be-cause I'd have been thinking only about throwing strikes. But once we got the two-run lead, it put a lot of pressure on them and helped me get those final four for the record. They were strug-gling and were swinging at a lot of borderline pitches from there on in.

It was great when I went back to the mound because the kid with the K cards was back and had put sixteen of them on the back wall of the bleachers. He hadn't been around since when I got hurt, but he was watching the game on NESN that night in Newton, got his mother to drive him down after the seventh, and got to the park in the bottom of the inning—right before Dwight's homer. When he had started lining up the cards in 1984 when I pitched, the ball club tried to stop him. But I told them to leave him alone. I like it. So what if it puts a little pressure on me? That's "Reggie pressure." Anyway, it puts pressure on the hitters too, be-cause they're thinking about it.

At that point, I was thinking about getting them out anyway. I didn't know about Bill Monbouquette's Red Sox record of seven-teen, but the third strike to Calderon did something crazy, and then I got Hendu for eighteen. When I passed out photographs of the twentieth strikeout to my teammates, I signed the one for Hender-

son: "without whom this night would never have been possible."
He laughed. Eighteen was my high, back at Spring Woods. I think
my top in college was fourteen, the minors fifteen, and my Red
Sox high had been the fifteen against Kansas City on August 21,
1984.

*Ninth Inning: Owen and Bradley struck out. Phelps grounded
to short. Twenty K's.* I was sitting up in the clubhouse between
innings with Nip, watching the game on TV. Nip said, "Now I can
tell you. Do you realize what you're doing? You need two strikeouts
for twenty and the record." I shrugged.

He repeated it as we went down the runway to start the inning,
and I guess a couple of guys told Nip that he shouldn't have put
the pressure on me. "He loves it," Nip shot back, and I guess they
were all into it when I started the inning. Hurst was leading a chant
of "one, two, three, blast-off" in time to my motion with each pitch.
That's how the nickname Rocket Man got started. They were doing
that "one, two, three, blast-off" stuff, and it caught on.

This time I got ahead of Spike; after he fouled one ball off down
the third base line, I got him to chase the high fastball. I got a strike
on Bradley, and to be honest, I don't know what was going through
his mind. He was in a slump at the time, but it was a tough year
for him against us. That time in May 1986 he charged the mound
in Seattle, Nipper dropped his left glove and landed a solid left cross
to his chin—a trick he had learned playing hockey—to protect
his pitching hand. Anyway, Bradley took the third strike, and I was
on my way to the Hall of Fame. It was great to look over to the
dugout and see all my teammates so into it, and Boggs—who later
said he spent a pleasant evening playing catch with Gedman—
brought the ball over, handed it to me, and simply said, "Awesome."
Phelps grounded to short, we had the 3–1 victory, and I was 4–0.

I felt tremendous that last inning, and I was told that Dave
Yochum, Toronto's advance scout, had me on the gun at 96 and
97 mph for all of my first six fastballs of the inning. Adrenaline
will do a lot. In the end, I threw 138 pitches (97 strikes).

After all the celebration on the field, I went over to the screen
and tried to give the ball to Deb, but she was afraid someone would
grab it away from her. So I kissed her and headed into the clubhouse.
When all the interviews were over, Nip again asked, "Do you realize
what you've done?"

"Yeah, but I want to go home and think about it and enjoy it,"

THE TWENTY-STRIKEOUT GAME: APRIL 29, 1986

Red Sox, 3-1

SEATTLE	ab	r	h	bi	BOSTON	ab	r	h	bi
Owen ss	4	0	1	0	DwEvns rf	4	1	2	3
Bradley lf	4	0	0	0	Boggs 3b	3	0	0	0
Phelps 1b	4	0	0	0	Bucknr dh	4	0	2	0
GThms dh	3	1	1	1	Rice lf	4	0	1	0
Presley 3b	3	0	0	0	Baylor 1b	3	0	1	0
Caldern rf	3	0	0	0	Stapltn 1b	0	0	0	0
Trtabll 2b	3	0	1	0	Gedman c	4	0	1	0
DHedsn cf	3	0	0	0	Barrett 2b	3	0	0	0
Yeager c	2	0	0	0	Lyons cf	3	1	1	0
Cowens ph	1	0	0	0	Hoffmn ss	2	0	0	0
Kearney c	0	0	0	0	Romero ss	0	1	0	0
Totals	**30**	**1**	**3**	**1**	**Totals**	**30**	**3**	**8**	**3**

Seattle			000	000	100–1
Boston			000	000	30x–3

Game-winning RBI – DwEvans (1).

E–Baylor, Tartabull, DP–Seattle 1. LOB–Seattle 2, Boston 7. 2B–Buckner. HR–GThomas (5), DwEvans (2). CS–Boston, Evans. Strikeouts–Seattle, Owen 2, Bradley 4, Phelps 3, Presley 2, Calderon 3, Henderson 3, Thomas, Tartabull, Yeager; Boston, Evans, Hoffman, Baylor 2, Barrett.

	IP	H	R	ER	BB	SO
Seattle						
MMoore (L 1-2)	7⅓	8	3	3	4	4
MYoung	⅓	0	0	0	0	0
Best	⅓	0	0	0	0	1
Boston						
Clemens (W 4-0)	9	3	1	1	0	20

Umpires–Home, Voltaggio; First, Welke; Second, Phillips; Third, McCoy
T–2.39 A–13,414

I told him. When I got home and started calling all my family, I kept saying, "I'm in the Hall of Fame." Nip also told me that before the game, Buckner had said, "He's got such great stuff tonight, he'll strike out eighteen." Buck should take Jimmy the Greek's place.

The next day was wild. I had a press conference, all kinds of telephone calls, and in a twenty-four-hour period had picture and interview sessions with *Time, People, Sports Illustrated, USA Today,* and places I'd never heard of. It was drizzling when I did the *SI* session; I had to pose three or four places, and it took nearly ninety minutes. When it was over, I thanked the photographer, Ron Modra.

"What are you thanking me for?" he asked.

"Hey, I enjoy this," I told him. "I've seen a lot of players try to stay away from publicity or the pressure. But when I was twelve, I wanted to be on the cover of *Sports Illustrated*, so I'm going to enjoy what's happening to me while I can."

NOTE: The numbers say that not only did Roger Clemens set a nine-inning record by breaking the twenty-strikeout barrier, only twenty-nine of the ninety-seven strikes he threw were even touched. Ten were put in play, nineteen were fouled off. Of the thirty batters he faced, on only five did he fail to get two strikes. "Looking at that box score the next day and seeing twenty strikeouts and no walks was one of the most astonishing things of my time in baseball," said California pitching coach Marcel Lachemann. In 111 seasons and more than 147,000 major league games, it had never been done. "That," said Boggs, "is all the perspective I need."

The previous record of nineteen was shared by Nolan Ryan (against the Red Sox) in 1974, Steve Carlton in 1969, Tom Seaver in 1970, and Providence's Charles Sweeney in 1884.

·5·
THE WINNING
STREAK

*"Sometimes I ask Roger if he realizes what he's doing,
and he doesn't. But I do. He's accomplishing history,
and it's fun having the locker next to his, watching
him and talking to him about it. Heck, the Red Sox
went from 1980 to 1985 without a starting pitcher
winning fourteen games, and he's won fourteen in a row."*
—*Al Nipper*

THE ATTENTION I enjoyed
and appreciated at first after breaking the strikeout record soon
became stressful. Magazines, newspapers, television and radio stations came pouring in from every small town in New England and
seemingly every big city around the country, and for the first time
I experienced some problems with the media. They didn't know
how I needed to stay on my program and work. I'm one of those
people who has to have his day planned from the moment I awake
in the morning, and I like to have my between-starts work schedule
planned to the minute. Deb says that if she asks me to hang a picture on the wall, I'll get a tape measure and make sure that it's
hung *exactly* in the middle. I'm not as precise as Chicken Man
(Boggs)—no one is—but I need to follow that program. I think that
if I start breaking down and letting a couple of things slide—OK,
today I'm not going to do these exercises or I'll skip the whirlpool—
that's how you get lazy and develop bad physical and psychological
habits. At times during the season, I tried to get this across to young
players such as Jeff Sellers, but I'm not sure it sank in, which I
can't understand. There's so much money to be made in this game,
why wouldn't one try to be in the best physical condition? I've
always understood why Randy as a coach became so frustrated with
kids who cheated themselves and their ability.

Anyway, after the twenty-strikeout game, I tried coming to the park an hour early, but still there was a line of people who each needed "only" ten or fifteen minutes. Dick Bresciani, Josh Spofford, and Jim Samia in the public relations department tried to screen people, but they couldn't tell someone from the *Los Angeles Times* that I don't have time. Unfortunately, it got a little out of hand, and some very good writers probably thought that I was being nonchalant or arrogant. But for fifteen days it became stressful, and I tried not to let my mind focus on the stress. It was bad in Boston for five days, and when we went out to the West Coast, every place I went they still wanted to hear it all again. Bresciani set up press conferences on the first day we'd go to each city, which helped, especially with my having to do something I don't do well—say no. At this point, the questions were still about coming back from the arm injury. Then, about the seventh win, my winning streak became the focal point.

At one point, on Friday, May 2, Channel 38 had Nip interview me; the piece was to be aired as the pregame show before my start against Oakland that Sunday. We had a little stunt set up (which Fish and Mac didn't go for because they were afraid that I'd burn my hand) for the end of the show. Nip said, "The ball still hasn't cooled off from the twenty-strikeout game, so let's go get 'em," and handed me the ball. It was soaked in lighter fluid and was supposed to be flaming, but the first time we tried it the flame went out. So we had to do the whole thing over. The assistant clubhouse man doused it in lighter fluid, and we did it again with it in flames—but he handed it to me quickly and I held it up with my right hand. I wasn't thinking. I should have grabbed it with my left hand. I am fortunate that I didn't burn myself.

As I got bombarded with all the individual questions, I tried hard to make sure that everything didn't come out I-me-my. It's a team game, and I can't win without my teammates, so when you're being asked one question after another about yourself, you have to be careful to deflect some of the glory back on them. I believe that's important, both for the sake of the team and my relationship with my teammates. If I don't have good teammates, I don't win. If I don't have teammates enjoying it with me, then it's no fun. Part of what makes this life so enjoyable and rewarding is the yearlong interaction among teammates, and I still think the best part of the twenty-strikeout game was looking over in the dugout and seeing how much the rest of the team was enjoying and sharing in what I'd done. That's the vivid picture that's frozen in my mind forever. No individual sport can match that feeling. I was named the American League player of the month for April, and by that time I had run out of words about myself.

When I finally got back out to pitch the Sunday afternoon following the April 29 game, it felt exciting. When I got two strikes on Athletics leadoff hitter Tony Phillips, the crowd was up and roaring. When I struck him out, the place went berserk. Nip and Charlie Moss told me they were talking about striking out twenty-one, and when I got Dwayne Murphy one and two, the fans were up and crazy again. I tried not to let the whole strikeout mania get to me, and it undoubtedly helped that we got four runs in the first inning, started by Evans' double. We won 4–1, I finished with a three-hitter and struck out ten (which tied fellow Texan Culp's Red Sox record of striking out ten or more in three consecutive games), and we were a half-game out of first place. The only run came on Dave Kingman's homer when he broke his bat. Jimmy went back to the wall as if it were a pop-up, and it scraped the top of the fence on its way down. Oh well, it would be the first of a few shutouts I'd miss because of gopher balls, and more important, we were off and running on a 12–2 streak that would eventually put us in first place to stay.

There was almost a feeling that I should be disappointed with ten strikeouts, and when I tried to close out other stuff, Nip, Hurst, and Can kept asking, "Do you know what you're doing?" It's tough to not know about it when you ride home with Nip every night for twenty minutes. He clicks through every stat and detail like a television commentator.

After that Oakland game May 4, we played two games with the Angels—Hurst shut out Witt 3–0 in one of them—that finished a 6–2 homestand, and we flew to the West Coast. We beat the Mariners there in two wild games. In the first one, Nip accidentally hit Bradley in the bill of the cap, and when he charged the mound, as I mentioned earlier, Nip resorted to his old hockey knowledge and dropped Bradley with a left cross to protect his pitching hand. The next night, Mike Brown stepped in and struck out eight and got the 4–2 victory when Rice and Baylor came up with big hits again in a four-run seventh. When the season was over, the starters, including Tom Seaver, got a lot of credit, but people forget that at different times during the year Brown, Sellers, Robbie Woodward, Stanley, and even Tim Lollar stepped in for starts and did excellent jobs that kept the team afloat.

My next start was Friday, May 9, in Oakland. I had a 5–2 lead in the ninth when I gave up singles to Kingman and Bruce Bochte, so McNamara decided to have Stanley finish it; after all, he had five straight saves at the time. Well, Carney Lansford took Stanley deep for a three-run homer that tied it, and Bob was so frustrated he and Coach Lachemann got into it. Bobby was so angry when he came in that he kicked the water cooler, broke it, and the water went all over Lach. "I didn't throw the damn pitch," Lachemann hollered, and they had a few words. It was no big deal. Stanley felt badly, but the important thing was that we came back and scored four runs in the tenth, and Sambito finished it up. That was a big win for us. Then Hurst pitched a tough, courageous ten-inning game on Saturday, and Can won on Sunday. The three-game sweep in Oakland moved us into first place for the first time.

We didn't stay on top. We went down to Anaheim and lost twice. Then my next start came up there on Wednesday, May 14, and I guess it will be remembered as the night that the 1986 Red Sox went into first place for good. That's an amazing thing to think about in retrospect—to go into first in the thirty-third game of the season and stay there for the last 129, especially in what may be the toughest division in baseball. If there was a game all season that I probably shouldn't have won, it was this one. Later in the season when I lost 1–0 to the White Sox on my birthday and someone consoled me about bad luck, I thought back to winning this one, 8–5. It was a game that was a struggle all night. The best thing that can be said about it was that I battled and battled all night because I didn't have close to my best stuff and was behind early. Reggie homered when I tried to quick pitch (thinking that the runner on first was going to go) and got the ball up. He crushed it. Hey, it was worth watching. Boggs hit a two-run homer, Gedman hit a three-run homer, Sambito saved me, and I survived five walks and a bad game because of my teammates. It was a short plane ride home. We were on top.

We came home to play Texas, which was becoming a tough team. Jose Guzman beat Hurst on May 16, despite Bruce's striking out fourteen; then Can won 8–2 on Saturday. But Sunday was the game where Nip got hurt. He was covering home plate when Larry Parrish came in and accidentally gashed him up pretty badly. Nip went down in a heap, and when we got out there, his knee was bleeding really badly and he was in terrible pain.

I saw the same fear in his eyes when he got ready to go to the hospital as I had felt in California the year before when I couldn't pitch and Nip sat with me in the hallway in Anaheim Stadium. I told Mac that I wanted to go with him, that he didn't have any family, and that he needed someone with him. So I went with him in the ambulance. I was able to help him settle down, which wasn't easy; he got really emotional at the time of the surgery. The doctor told him it wasn't career ending, and that while it was a deep and serious laceration, he had missed severing everything in his knee by an inch or two. I stayed right on through the night. When he woke up and others came in to see him, I checked out. Friends are awfully important, and friends wash the blood off other friends' toes when they need it. Especially in a business like ours.

The game itself was funny. We were trying to listen in the ambulance, and then we watched the ending in Nip's room. That was the play where Marty hit a ball into right field, and George Wright of the Rangers dived for it. Lyons thought it had been caught, so he tagged up and met Marty at second. They both ended up scoring in a comedy, when Wright's throw went through everyone and into the dugout. That made Nip laugh. Ole Psycho (Lyons) is baseball's human highlight film when he gets on the bases. We never knew if he liked the name Psycho or not, but he had it on a sign over his locker and never seemed to get too upset about it, so the name stuck.

Nip and I have been friends since my rookie year, but it was during the surgery and the hospital stay that we were closest. The relationships that I've experienced with him and with Bruce are two things in this game that will never be lost. There are so many natural jealousies that we all saw when we came up that relationships without any jealousies are irreplaceable. I think about Nip with me in the tunnel in California. I also remember Bruce and me sitting in the trainer's room in the fifth game of the play-offs saying to each other, "It's not time for this season to end." I'll remember those things more than some strikeout number twenty years from now.

The relationship with Nipper began because we both liked to go to the park early and work out when we're on the road. He liked to run, and jumped in with my program, although he's got such great legs that he's more of a distance runner than I am. The best thing about him is his attitude. He's got that competitiveness. Anything I do, he tries to do better with friendly competitiveness. We have driving contests on the way home and will take all sorts of back roads en route to Malden to try to win. We pump each other all the time, and players need constant pumping whether they admit it or not. Nip does, too. He's a worrier. He's always worried that the Red Sox are going to trade him. In the winter, he calls all the time; no wonder he got that ulcer. This past winter, he called all excited because he'd read in the St. Louis paper that the Sox had offered him and Henderson for Willie McGee. I just told him not to worry, that he couldn't do anything about it and anyone in baseball would want a twelve- or fourteen-game winner.

He's a fan. He claims he went to every one of Seaver's starts in St. Louis in the seventies. He's also read twenty-five or thirty books on pitching and is constantly looking for ideas. In one book, he read about Steve Carlton's doing exercises through a huge container of rice, which strengthens one's forearms. I started doing it and liked it. That is, until one day we found out that two kids of a couple of the players had urinated in the rice. That killed that program for a while.

Some players get on Nip about hanging around with me, but he's just having fun. If we're in a restaurant and adults interrupt our dinner asking for autographs, he politely asks them to leave; one time in New York a man wasn't polite, so Nip aired him out and asked him, "Don't you have any couth?" It was funny. He loves to live the life of the bachelor, and when a reporter told him in spring training that he had heard he was engaged, Nip demanded that he "kill that rumor as fast as possible." One night we were at a Celtics game and the public address announcer asked if we would mind being introduced. I was in the process of saying, "I don't think it would be a good idea, this is their game," and Nip told him where our seats were and said we'd love to be announced. That cracked me up.

The Red Sox were on a roll when they won the May 18 game with the Rangers. The next night we were down 7–5 to Minnesota in the eighth inning and scored one in that inning. Then in the ninth, with two out and two on, we watched Ron Davis walk Buckner to load the bases, walk Rice to tie it at 7–7, and hit Sullivan to win it. We had games all season where we were down in the seventh or eighth inning and we just knew we'd come back and win it. In that Minnesota game, Davis was out of control, and someone—Barrett or Nip, probably—predicted that he'd hit Sullivan to end it. That's when you know you're doing well.

We call Barrett the computer who wore tennis shoes or, better, the computer who wore spikes. He must sit at home thinking of statistics and little angles, but he's on top of everything during games. Lachemann works hours and hours before and after games keeping charts on opposing hitters, and Marty loves those things. He probably plays hitters as well as anyone in the league, too. He'll miss Lach now that he's left to coach in Oakland. A lot of people will miss him, because he is one of the hardest working people around. He and Walter Hriniak will never get paid what they deserve. And as far as I'm concerned, Fischer is great, too. But he gets very nervous about things. On a day I'm starting, he'll tell me ten or twenty times, "7:10 in the bull pen, got it?" Nip and I would play games with him. "They've got some ceremony before the game, so it's not going to start until 7:50 instead of 7:35," one of us would say. Fish would get flustered and start pounding in that catcher's glove he carries around. "Nobody told me; what the heck's going on?" he'd bark, and head into Mac's office. But he's great on mechanics, and he's done a terrific job teaching pitchers to hold runners on. He teaches slide steps, quick pitches, holding the ball to make base stealers lose their rhythm, and it all works. The first seventeen guys who ran on me my rookie year stole successfully. This entire season, only twenty-one runners tried to steal on me, and Gedman threw out fourteen of them.

My winning streak got to 8–0 on May 20, when I held on for a 17–7 victory over the Twins. That was actually one of the toughest games to pitch, especially in Fenway. I had a six-run lead in the first inning, and keeping my concentration and competitiveness isn't easy in a runaway. I just tried to throw strikes; I didn't walk anyone, but I also gave up two homers. The dangerous thing in Fenway is that if you get too careless, a ten-run lead can disappear.

We finished a three-game sweep of Minnesota for a two-game lead and then headed for Texas, where I was going to pitch the third of another three-game series on May 25. I had had this date circled for weeks. Deb, my mother, three sisters, Richard, Deb's parents, and assorted friends were all there at the Arlington Sheraton Center. I was talking to Bonnie at the pool, and Sambito asked me who she was. "My little sister," I told him. "This is Texas, all right," he replied; "I hope my son grows up to be as big." Teammates kidded me that everywhere they went around the hotel, there was a Clemens or a relative or a friend. It was fun. It was also exhausting.

Can had pitched a great game to win the opener, we'd lost the second, and when I went out on Sunday afternoon, it was a perfect day for me. It was hot and humid, and I knew right away that I had good stuff. All during this streak, McNamara and Fischer were telling reporters that every time I go out to the mound I have a chance for a no-hitter, and I almost got one before the home folks that day. I got to two outs in the eighth inning before Oddibe McDowell hit a single out of the reach of a great diving try by Lyons.

I got to about the sixth inning before I even realized that I had a no-hitter going, so it was then that I started to think about it. I had gone through four and five without knowing it, but after a couple of outs in the sixth, I realized that I hadn't given up a hit. Or so I thought. I also knew that everyone was being quiet. I glanced up at the scoreboard, and sure enough, I had one going. When we were hitting in the eighth, I tried to sit as far away from everyone as possible, as I knew that no one was going to say anything to me, anyway. I switched shirts and sat down, and Buckner sat down and whispered to Boggs, "You know, he's got a no-no going." I heard him. Then I knew I was in trouble. Boggs, the master of superstition, looked down and then glanced at me and knew that I had heard Buck. So I reached down and tied two knots in my shoe. I should have tied six, because I got two outs in the eighth when McDowell got the hit. I always tell people that I'm not superstitious, but I never step on foul lines, I'm very careful on full moons . . . but I'm not superstitious. I guarantee that every player is superstitious about something. Not quite like Boggs, but everyone has superstitions about something.

I'd faced McDowell three times when he was at Arizona State. (Actually, the person I had been most worried about was Toby Harrah, because he was on every pitch and hit the ball hard every time.) Oddibe hit the line drive, and Lyons—in as a defensive replacement —made a heck of a try, but couldn't get to it. In the ninth, I gave up a homer to Darrell Porter to spoil the shutout, 7–1. Here I was 8–0 and leading the league in earned run average, and I'd given up at least one homer in every one of my nine starts.

The strange thing in that game was that I hurt my knuckle. My fingers bent back on one certain pitch, and it started swelling up. I did it in the first or second inning, it started swelling, and I thought it would affect my control. In fact, I seriously wondered if I was going to be able to continue. The ball turned in my hand. Charlie Moss kept putting that freezing spray on it and that numbed it so much that I couldn't even feel it by the seventh or eighth inning, and I got by. It stemmed from an old Spring Woods football injury. I got my hand caught in a face mask tackling a guy, and when he went down, my finger twisted. All I got for my efforts were a penalty and a cracked knuckle.

The Red Sox sent me home to Boston, so I had to miss the Cleveland series. Dr. Pappas said the knuckle had been broken in the past, but it had healed and all I did was shift it. It took a few days for it to stop hurting, so I stayed home. That meant that I watched the so-called fog game on television. That was the night the game was stopped in the sixth inning because of heavy fog, so we won 2–0. We won it when Mel Hall hit a shot into the fog, Armas saw it off the bat, guessed where it would go, ran back to the fence, and when it came down out of the fog, speared it. With almost anyone else, it would have been an inside-the-park, three-run homer, but Tony has instincts for the game that amaze me. (He easily was the best base runner on the team, and he's a lot faster than people think.) I have no idea how he saw that ball, because we couldn't see him on television, but it saved us. The funniest thing about that game was that afterward Can said, "That's what they get for building a stadium on the ocean." Can was a sociology, not geography, major at Jackson State.

I rejoined the team in Minnesota on May 30. Since my start had been backed up two days, Woodward had a chance to start that night. The second game (May 31) was the night Hurst got hurt. He was rolling along on another strong, easy win and had thrown the last pitch of the fifth inning. I was following the flight of the ball, so I didn't see him do it. When I looked up, he was writhing on the ground in unbelievable pain. I thought it must have been his elbow at first. Then when we rushed out there, we found out he'd done something to his groin. I discovered through him that groin injuries can almost be as bad as arm. The muscle was torn off the bone so badly that they said they could stick a thumb in there and there'd be a gap. We'd heard about Louie Sleigher of the Bruins and how he'd been out for almost two years with a groin injury, and a pitcher uses the same upper leg muscles pushing off as hockey players do. If it had been anywhere else on his body, he still could have pitched. But that was his push-off leg, and we knew it would be a longer process than the ten days that someone estimated. We carried him off as best as we could, but the pain was grabbing him terribly until they numbed him with ice. The injury nagged him and nagged him, and naturally he was worried about getting all screwed up when he tried to come back, which could have happened if he got his mechanics out of whack. Bruce didn't feel as if he was pushing off right when he started throwing on the side. We watched films day after day until he got all his confidence back to push off the mound. It took him a few starts to get that confidence back. He did a ton of throwing on the side, but many times when he tried to hump up, he'd grab. He asked me to come out early and watch him. It was a long, tough process.

Hurst's injury was a big loss for us. Sammy Stewart got hurt in the same game, so in a period of less than two weeks we'd lost Nipper, Hurst, and Stewart. Bruce was 5–3 at the time, but he was our best pitcher in May and leading the league in strikeouts. His forkball had become a dominant strikeout pitch for him. Actually, we had learned that pitch together. In August 1984, we originally were shown what to do by Roger Craig, the professor of the split-finger and forkball. Later we got another important lesson from Mike Boddicker one day when we were all standing around in the outfield in Baltimore. Bruce and I both throw a forkball. With the forkball, you jam the ball between the fingers. With the split-finger, you just spread your fingers farther apart in your grip. Nolan Ryan throws a split-finger that he can run away from lefties. I threw a forkball at Texas, but I had my thumb on the bottom of the ball and I never could control it. Then I found out how the thumb is supposed to go on the side, and it's starting to come around. I hope it will be a big pitch for me in time.

It was important that we were still ahead in the standings when we lost all those pitchers. If we'd been behind at that point, I think it would have been difficult to catch someone with two starters hurt. We were up by three. I kept saying, "I sure like being here better than being three games out," and that took some of the heat off. It was true, too, because in other years we were always the third-place team trying to catch the second-place team, and we'd come up short.

The knuckle was still bothering me on June 1, when I pitched against the Twins, but Baylor hit another homer and all I gave up in eight innings was a two-run homer to Roy Smalley. I had some problems with my mechanics early, but got them back. It was funny throughout the season. I had more periods than I ever remember where I'd go three or four innings in seven or eight starts and I'd fight myself and couldn't get any rhythm. Maybe it was my being tense. Every game you win in this kind of streak, the pressure builds more and more. By that game in Minnesota, I was thinking about the streak. My goal had been to get off to a 4–1 or 5–1 start. Then once I got to 8–0, my goal was to get to 10–0. I got there, and my goal was simply to prepare for the start in New York and beat the Yankees on June 16, because they were right on our tails and the media was already pointing at that series.

In the meantime, we went home from Minneapolis to sweep the Indians for a 4½ game lead, then went to Milwaukee. I'll never forget the first game there, June 5. We were losing 7–5 in the ninth, there were two outs, Mark Clear was pitching, Boggs hitting, and Lyons was on second and Barrett on first. Now, you don't have to give Psycho much encouragement to take off, and from what I heard, Marty said, "If you can make it safely, go." We were down two runs, and Marty wanted to get into scoring position with Boggs at the plate, and anyway, Clear wasn't paying any attention. So off went Lyons. Psycho told me afterward that when he heard the umpire call him out, it was like the end of *The Longest Yard*—when they snapped the ball and it all turned into slow motion. He heard the umpire say "outoutoutoutoutout," echo after echo after echo. He looked up, and it seemed as if the umpire were in slow motion calling him out. He said his heart went right through his feet, and if he could have dressed in the dugout, he would have. (In Milwaukee, the manager dresses right there in the clubhouse with the players.) We had a little cool-down period, and the locker room was very quiet. Poor Psycho. McNamara said it was one of the dumbest plays he'd ever seen, and benched him. Looking back, it was one of those crazy games that made the season so much fun, even if we did lose. We never did the same thing twice when we stepped on the field.

Psycho means well, he just has a way of doing wild and crazy things. After he was traded to the White Sox, I read where their manager, Jim Fregosi, said, "What Lyons does best is look in the stands and give television interviews," and then sent him to Buffalo. When he left us, Baylor said, "There goes half our Kangaroo Court fund." The Judge got Psycho for talking to other players, talking into the stands, having his hat off . . . everything. The court was a great thing. Someone would file a charge, Baylor would write it down, and we'd have a court hearing in the clubhouse. There were automatic fines for hitters failing to move runners over or pitchers giving up hits on 0–2 pitches. Among other things, we'd get fined for stupid plays or fraternization with the enemy. I got hit for 0–2 pitches, and one time in September for talking to Hearon in Toronto. However, one time I appealed and won. (If you appealed and lost, the fine was doubled to $50.) I had been charged with eating candy right before a game in Seattle in May. As you leave the clubhouse and go through the hallway to the dugout, the clubhouse man has a huge rack of candy. But I'm not a junk food eater; the only thing I eat off that rack are the granola bars, and I was falsely accused that night. So I won the appeal. That was about the only time the Judge reversed his decision. After the All-Star Game we took the pot and had a catered party in Seattle. But as the second half of the season went along, the court died out a little. I know it did a lot to lighten the air of the clubhouse and turn our attention to little things, but Psycho must have lost a third of his salary.

I got my tenth win the night after Psycho's base-running adventure, and it turned out to be my only shutout of the season, 3–0. When I finished the game, I went over and hugged Fish and said, "I kept the ball in the ballpark." I had four starts at that point where I lost shutouts because of solo homers and had allowed at least one home run in each of the ten previous starts. The Brewers started six left-handed hitters against me, and they were all trying to hit the ball down the left field line. Rice was playing them perfectly, hugging the line, so what would have been doubles were all easy outs, even if a couple of them were hit pretty hard. It doesn't really bother me to have a lineup stacked with left-handers. Now that I have two different fastballs, if I have my curveball going, I'm all

Roger celebrates winning the first of many titles and awards, as his team at the University of Texas has just clinched the 1983 college world series title. (Photo courtesy of the Sports Information Office, University of Texas)

The UT Longhorns' 1983 pitching staff: below Roger is Calvin Schiraldi, who would also pitch on the 1986 Red Sox team, and flanking Roger are Mike Capel (his right) and Kirk Killingsworth. (Photo courtesy of the Sports Information Office, University of Texas)

At the 1986 World Series, the "Austin Red Sox"—Roger, Spike Owen, and Calvin Schiraldi—pose with their UT coaches, Cliff Gustafson (right) and Bill Bethen. (Photo courtesy of the Sports Information Office, University of Texas)

Two keys to the Pawtucket Red Sox starting rotation stand together on opening day 1984; with Roger is Rich Gale. (Photo courtesy of the Pawtucket Red Sox)

After being called up from Pawtucket in 1984, Roger's rookie year with the Boston Red Sox included retrieving the balls as well as throwing them. (Photo by Peter Travers)

Roger's first full season began with spring training 1986 and a lot of throwing for rehab from his shoulder injury and operation. Here, pitching coach Bill Fischer looks on, in Osceola, Florida. (Photo by Joe Hickey)

Rocket Roger. (Photo by Peter Travers)

During Roger's record-breaking twenty-strikeout game against the Seattle Mariners on April 29, 1986, the nineteenth strikeout—to tie the record—was former UT teammate Spike Owen. Later in the season, Spike was traded to the Red Sox. (Photo by Joe Hickey)

The twentieth strikeout. (Photo by Joe Hickey)

The team congratulates
Roger after the
twentieth strikeout.
(Photo by Peter Travers)

Roger's wife, Debbie,
also offers her
congratulations.
(Photo by Peter Travers)

From April through June 1986, Roger ran up a fourteen-game winning streak. It came to an end on July 2, when he suffered his first loss. This picture, taken on July 1, seems to presage the next day's events. (Photo by Peter Travers)

To Debbie and Roger Clemens
Congratulations on the 20K Game, Ronald Reagan

Following Roger's visit to the White House, President Reagan sent him this personalized photograph. Roger has just handed the President a game ball from his twenty-strikeout game. (White House photo by Pete Souza)

Roger runs sprints with fellow-pitcher Bruce Hurst. (Photo by Peter Travers)

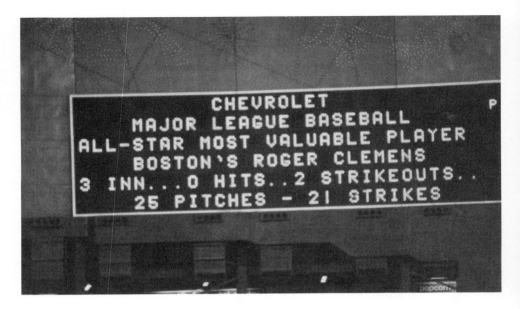

CHEVROLET   P
MAJOR LEAGUE BASEBALL
ALL-STAR MOST VALUABLE PLAYER
BOSTON'S ROGER CLEMENS
3 INN...0 HITS..2 STRIKEOUTS..
25 PITCHES - 21 STRIKES

In mid-July, one of Roger's goals was reached: he started and was the winning pitcher of the All-Star Game. He also won the MVP Award. At left, he signs autographs before the game. (Photos by Joe Hickey)

Al Nipper interrupts a postgame interview with a bottle of champagne. On this occasion—August 30, 1986—Roger has just won his twentieth game of the season. (Photo by Joe Hickey)

Al Nipper (#49) and Rich Gedman (#10) hug Oil Can Boyd following their September 28 game clinching the division title. Roger heads toward the group with his arms outstretched. (Photo by Joe Hickey)

Roger's version of a victory lap following the division clinch: astride a policeman's horse. (Photo courtesy of the Boston Red Sox)

CLEMENS

W-L	24-4
IP	254.0
SO	238
ERA	2.48

Roger's numbers at the end of the 1986 season. (Photo by Joe Hickey)

Geddy and Manager McNamara meet with Roger at the mound in the first game of the play-offs; uncharacteristically, Roger struggled from the start in that game and never really found his groove. The Sox lost, 8–1. (Photo courtesy of the Boston Red Sox)

The K cards that were Roger's trademark throughout the season multiplied during the play-offs. (Photo courtesy of the Boston Red Sox)

In the seventh game of the Championship Series, Roger pitched seven innings of shutout baseball, earning his first win in three postseason starts. The Angels were never in the game, and the Sox won the pennant by the same score that they had lost the first game of the series: 8–1. (Photo courtesy of the Boston Red Sox)

The World Series win seemed a moment away in the not-to-be-forgotten sixth game, in New York. Roger pitched a no-hitter for the first four innings, but then things got complicated. The Mets won, ultimately, 6–5 in the tenth and went on to take the crown in the seventh game. (Photo courtesy of the Boston Red Sox)

The park erupted with applause when these balloons fell in Fenway during the fourth game of the World Series, as the home crowd expressed a season's worth of love and appreciation for a team that gave them one of the most exciting years ever. (Photo courtesy of the Boston Red Sox)

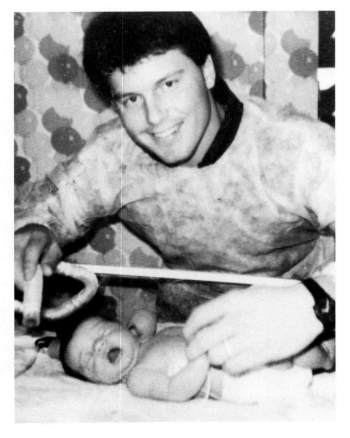

In December, Roger's first child arrived: Koby Aaron. When asked about the name, Roger replied, "You knew there would be a 'K' in there someplace!" (Wide World Photos)

right. [Left-handed batters hit .212 against Clemens for the season, right-handers .174.]

We lost three out of four in Milwaukee, then moved on to Toronto. Mike Stenhouse was the hero of the second game there, when he walked with the bases loaded in the tenth inning, which made everyone happy. Stenhouse was a popular guy and, even though he'd never caught, was a bull pen catcher and part of the Savings and Loan Association that Stewart thought up. They had Stewart, Stanley, Sambito, (Dave) Stapleton, and Stenhouse with names starting with *S*, Lollar with an *L*; they saved, and they loaned Lollar out for one start. The management got down on Sammy as the season wore along, and there was a bad incident with Jack Rogers (where Stewart was accused of spitting in the traveling secretary's face), but he was a funny man who kept the bull pen and clubhouse loose. I know he was late sometimes, but his two children have multiple sclerosis, and Sammy has to spend a lot of time with them. I don't think any of us can appreciate what it's like to go through what the Stewarts do every day of their lives.

My start in Toronto, on June 11, was the third game of the series, and it was a nasty night—cold, rain, and wind. I warmed up three times in the rain. They said the game was going to start on time, so I warmed up, only to have to go into the clubhouse and put a heat pack on my shoulder for forty-five minutes. Fischer was going crazy. He had a cold and was hacking, and he was angry about the conditions; I guess they had a big advance ticket sale. When I threw, I made sure I didn't throw too much, so I kept my legs if the game actually started. Because of the adversity of the conditions, when it did start—two hours and forty-seven minutes late—it had become a serious challenge and probably helped me. That was, however, the first time I put that atomic bomb heat on my body. I'm allergic to menthol, so I broke out everywhere; but Charlie Moss told me I had a choice between my skin breaking out or my shoulder stiffening up. I took the skin problem. Baylor [who batted .302 in Clemens starts] hit a homer, Stanley pitched the ninth, and we won, 3–2. That put my winning streak at eleven. Afterward, Toronto starter Doyle Alexander blasted the Blue Jays' management for being money hungry in starting the game.

We went home and lost two out of three to the Brewers—my old buddy Tim Leary beat us for the second of three times—so we went to New York on June 16, having lost 6 out of 10 and with the Yankees only 3½ games behind us. When we arrived in New York, it was built up to be the series that meant everything. We were supposed to collapse and fold. I think a lot of people thought that we'd be very nervous and tense, but in reality we were very excited. We thought it was going to be fun.

And it was. Ron Guidry and I were matched up in the opener, so there was tremendous anticipation of that game. The momentum was immediately ours. We put the hurt on Guidry pretty quickly, with Rice knocking in two runs in the top of the first, which was pretty big. I knew that I *had* to go shut them down, and it started right. I struck out Rickey Henderson with a slider, and as he walked away he bowed and said something to me. Guidry got knocked out in the third, and we rolled to a 10–1 win that was a show. There were fights all over the stands, and we read in the paper the next day that owner George Steinbrenner had made a bunch of calls downstairs. Mattingly was quoted as saying, "We can't spit blood every day." What a place. The next night Evans hit two homers and we held on for a wild 7–6 victory. Mac pulled two pitchers out in the middle of counts, Rice threw Butch Wynegar out at the plate to save it, and poor Geddy got hurt in about five different places. There's never a dull moment in Yankee Stadium, because we read the next day that Billy Martin had ripped Don Zimmer ("the third base coach lost this game") on television and that Steinbrenner had called Manager Lou Piniella and demanded an organizational meeting the next afternoon.

But that afternoon before the game was one of the toughest scenes I'd ever witnessed. I'd just gotten into the clubhouse off the subway. A lot of players were outside, hitting, and all of a sudden I saw Charlie and Mac going in and out of the trainer's room. Boggs had gotten a call there and was told that his mother had been killed in an automobile accident. He went into shock and was on the floor, all crouched up. It was terrifying. I thought about how I would have reacted, and I doubt I could have played for the rest of the season, but he returned a week later. The month after was one of the worst of his career, but that's by his standards; it was good by anyone else's, and this was just another reason to respect the man.

I watch Boggs continually. I don't know if he realizes how much I watch him and admire what he does, but when I go out under the center field stands and do my sit-ups, I stop and watch what he does in the cage. Incredible. He arrives at the park at the same time every day, goes through the same dressing routine every day, takes a hundred ground balls at the same time, goes out to center field and meditates at the same time, runs at the same time. . . . He works at everything. I swear he'd rather win a gold glove for his defense than a silver bat for his offense. When Calvin and Wes Gardner came over from the Mets, all they talked about was "Keith Hernandez this and Keith Hernandez that." Hernandez is a great hitter and worker, too. But I told them, "Just take a week and watch Boggs." It didn't even take a week. Calvin watched him for four or five days, and he couldn't believe it. Oh and two? It seems like he'd rather hit there. He'll get down two strikes and guys on the bench will yell, "You're in trouble now." [Boggs swung at and missed only forty-six pitches over the entire season.] Everyone *talks* about being mentally prepared, but guys like Boggs and Mattingly do it, day after day. Boggs is also incredibly competitive. He wins almost every home run hitting contest he plays in.

We were all stunned and shaken by the Boggs incident, but we finished a three-game sweep in Yankee Stadium when Can pitched a tough 5–2 one in the third game. Baylor won it with a three-run double in the ninth, which meant a lot to him after all his problems with Steinbrenner. He had tears in his eyes when he talked to the press in the clubhouse, and he said, "Tonight, we have become a *team.*" Steinbrenner was so angry that he said, "Baylor's bat will be dead by August." Wrong, again.

When we got home to Boston, the town was really excited. The Orioles scored fourteen runs against us the first night (June 20), but there were 35,707 in Fenway the next afternoon, when I started on national television. We got four runs in the first inning off Ken Dixon, and while I didn't have my best start, it was a relatively easy 7–2 win. Geddy said he knew I wasn't sharp because he had to move his glove. The next morning, I read a Baylor quote: "I went against Guidry in 1978 when he was absolutely overpowering, day after day. I went against Vida Blue in 1971 when he was packing them in everywhere. I played with Nolan Ryan, Jim Palmer, Dave McNally . . . and Clemens stands alone on what he brings to a team on the day that he pitches." Coming from the Judge, that's a compliment it will be hard to forget. It made my 13–0 streak [which made Clemens the seventh pitcher ever to win his first thirteen games] better.

When we lost the first two games of our Yankee series in Fenway the next week (June 23–24) and our lead dropped back to four games, it seemed people got pretty nervous again. The first two games were 11–3 and 8–1 routs, and we didn't know who was going to pitch the finale. Nip was ready to come back at that point. He'd been throwing some on the side, and was supposed to report to Pawtucket that day to begin his twenty-day rehabilitation. However, he and Mac and Fish decided that he could come back and start, and it turned out to be a big lift to the entire team. We got five runs in the first inning and knocked out Doug Drabek, and Nip battled with all his guts for seven innings to hold off the Yankees, who were hot at the time. Sambito came in and struck out the side in the eighth. When Henderson reached base to lead off the ninth, Joe picked him off and preserved the 5–4 win.

Then came Baltimore. The Orioles had beaten us two out of three in Fenway the previous weekend, and when Mac sent me out to open the series, there were 52,159—the second largest crowd they've ever drawn for a regular season game—in Memorial Stadium. For the first time since May 14, I got behind 1–0, giving up the first of Eddie Murray's two homers. But I got into a good rhythm, retired fifteen out of sixteen after the second-inning homer, and we scored three in the sixth. Armas homered in the seventh for a 4–1 lead that produced a 5–3 win, getting our lead back to six games. Actually, it was tough facing a strong lineup like the Orioles have twice in a week, and it might have helped if I had thrown fewer strikes. The second time around, good hitters like theirs know what to expect and are more comfortable at the plate. But we won, and Oil Can and Sellers won the next two games, so our lead was up to eight games.

And my streak was 14–0. Every day I read about records (only Rube Marquard's nineteen, Elroy Face's seventeen, and Johnny Allen and Dave McNally's fifteen game streaks were better, and ironically, the postgame press conference that day in Baltimore was held in front of McNally's former locker). I was trying to stay unemotional, although it's hard when you're being told you're going for an American League record in your next start. I read in the paper where Dick Howser said I was going to start the All-Star Game. I read about MVP, Cy Young, thirty wins. . . . "All I'm thinking about is number fifteen," I kept telling reporters.

Actually, the second night in Baltimore my mind was taken off the streak. It was about three in the morning when the phone rang, waking me. It was Nip, all excited.

"We just got Tom Seaver." I thought I was dreaming, and told him so.

"No, man. We got Seaver. This is it."

"Who'd we give up?"

"Psycho." I called Lyons to wish him luck.

The next morning, the *Boston Globe*'s headline read, "Seaver Finally Changes His Sox." Nip was beside himself. He was going to pitch with his idol. Seaver had sat down with him in the outfield in Chicago when Nip was a rookie. Then it was one of his biggest thrills when he got to start against him on national television. I'd always watched him, too, because his leg drive was so important.

I had no idea what to expect in Tom Seaver, but when we got back to Boston, our lockers were right next to one another. He came in quietly. When he wasn't pitching, he was studying every other pitcher like he had a microscope. He was also very close to Fischer and McNamara, and he told us that Fischer was unique in his ability to spot tiny mechanical flaws in Tom's delivery. After we won the opener of the Toronto series at Fenway, he was going to make his Boston debut the night before I went for my fifteenth. I had to chart the game, and I couldn't believe how confusing it was. He's extremely hard to chart because it's so difficult to tell what he's throwing. He changes speeds so many different ways on his fastball. His slider is so tight and has such a quick, two- or three-inch tight break that it's hard to differentiate it from a cut fastball. Gedman would just call a fastball, and Tom would throw what he wanted. Sometimes it would be a mediocre fastball, almost a change-up. Then sometimes he'd bust it up there at 90 or 91. I didn't have any idea of what he was throwing half the time. The only way to chart him is to go upstairs and do it off the camera.

Then came my turn with the Blue Jays—and the try for the American League record, July 2. I'd done my routine between starts, studied some tapes and tried to concentrate on breaking the game down into innings. I wanted to make certain that I shut them down in the top of the first, and when I got out there, I knew that I had great stuff. Toronto's left-hander Jimmy Key shut us down, as well, and it was obvious that it was going to be a tough game. I gave up a homer to George Bell in the fourth, which angered me; it's important to shut down the opposition in that inning also. But

Barrett, Mr. Clutch, hit a two-run homer in the fifth, and while I walked two guys in the seventh, I was under one hundred pitches and went into the eighth with a 2–1 lead and a one-hitter.

There I made my biggest mistake. I walked catcher Ernie Whitt leading off the inning. Then I got Damaso Garcia 0 and 2, didn't get a fastball far enough outside, and he dumped a single into right field. We nailed Whitt at third on Tony Fernandez's bunt. Rance Mulliniks was the next hitter, a good dead high fastball hitter. I made a good pitch to him, a fastball that was running away. He didn't even get around on it; he simply stuck his bat out and sliced a ball down the left field line that landed near the corner for a double. That tied it at 2–2 and left runners at second and third. I immediately started thinking about Lloyd Moseby, their third hitter, against whom I'd had pretty decent success in the past.

I turned around and saw Mac coming to the mound. I thought that he was coming out to talk, not to come get me and yank me out of the game. When he asked for the ball and said Stanley was coming in, I couldn't believe it, but I didn't say anything because I was at the point where I needed to go be by myself to cool down. As it turned out, Stanley gave up the two runs [relievers allowed five of Clemens' runs to score all year, four in two games with Stanley], and we lost 4–2. The streak was over.

Randy called me after the game, screaming; and I'll have to admit, I felt I should have been left in there. In the first place, I can get out of trouble [the opposition batted .143 against him in clutch situations with runners in scoring position]. I was still throwing the ball well; no one had pulled a ball in the air against me the entire game. A streak like that comes along once in a lifetime, and I believed that I'd earned the right that one night to win or lose my own game rather than be taken out with no chance to win and a good chance to lose. I told reporters, "Now I hope all the media can go back to their homes and come back to see us in August, when we're still playing well," but I was very disappointed. In the next day or two, Mac and I sat down and talked it out so he would know that if a game was on the line, I wanted to be out there. But if we had more than a three-run lead after the seventh, I was going to be out of there, because we were starting the crunch and homestretch.

I had some sort of a letdown, because my next start (July 7) against Oakland, was the low point of my season. I was very sluggish. The intensity wasn't there. I wasn't the same person, sort of down. In the sixth inning, Jose Canseco hit a slider into the screen, then Kingman took a weird swing—he didn't even stride, he just pushed a pitch in his eyes into the night—and it was 6–1. I'd gotten us into a hole, and we lost 6–4.

Deb could see the distress that was raging in me as I walked off the mound. She hadn't seen me like that in a while, so she knew something was wrong. I came in and threw some stuff around the clubhouse, angry because the game was all my fault because I wasn't excited or keyed up or simply ready to do my job. I was trying to manufacture energy and excite myself. What I'd done after the Toronto game was let down and relax. Nobody was in front of my locker for the first time in two months, and I let the air out a little. When I got to the clubhouse, I knew I'd just wasted a chance to go out there and pitch, which meant I'd let down my teammates and myself. I get only thirty-four opportunities to pitch, and I'd just thrown one away. I'd ripped my jersey buttons off, and Deb was at the back door of the clubhouse.

"You want to run?" she asked.

"I'm tempted to sit here in the hallway and try to kill myself with five hundred sit-ups."

She's amazing. She always knows when I need to talk and when I need to run. I think it helped that she is such an outstanding athlete herself. She played powder-puff football, she caught in softball, she's an outstanding rider, great at racquetball . . . when I was going through arm rehab, she caught me at 70–75 miles per hour. She's seen me in minor league games; she even saw me back in high school and watched Texas games on television. My rookie year in six or seven starts she completely appreciated how much pressure there was. We were dating and engaged then, but she understood that there's a time for fun and there's a time to be serious. She's almost like my second pitching coach. I got my first big league shutout against Chicago with an eight-hitter, and she told me I gave up too many hits, too many walks. "That's not you," she told me. Nip got all over her, but she *was* right. Now she keeps pitching charts and will tell me that some guy hit a fastball twice in a row.

Deb knows the frustrations I go through, she understands pressure. Even this winter, after Koby was born and I'd had awards pouring in, she kept saying, "Work harder, this is going to be a tougher season." We're both from similar backgrounds, we've both worked hard for everything we've had. The only thing that gets me is that she thinks Larry Bird is the best athlete in the country, no matter what. Of all the things I won, when the magazine *The Fan* named me co-MVP of the 1986 year in New England with Bird, she was happiest. "That," she told me, "means something." Nice.

Anyway, she instinctively knew what I needed after the Athletics knocked me out that night. She went into the weight room with me, then the next thing I knew she told the parking lot guy to get my car out. I put on my running stuff, and she drove me over to the Charles, by the bridge to Harvard Square. I ran down to the Massachusetts Avenue Bridge while she drove alongside me. I did one hundred sit-ups, ran back, did one hundred more. It was strange running along the river, looking up and seeing the lights of the Fenway and seeing Boston from the side. It allowed me to step away, while letting off some of my frustrations. I finished my sit-ups and got back into the car. "You had no life to you," she said, and she was right. She said there was no change in the game, and we drove back to the park.

I had to go back to the clubhouse and answer questions, but by then I was in the right frame of mind to handle them. I showered, went and told Fish and Mac that I was fine and was ready to go in my next start. And I was, too. By the time I was back at the park, the blahs were gone and I was focusing on my one last start before the All-Star Game. Don't ever let anyone tell you wives can't be a big part of success.

·6·
THE ALL-STAR
GAME AND AFTER

*"Roger Clemens is a very exciting pitcher. My first
impression? That he's going to have a long and
successful career. All I know is that he throws harder
than anyone I've seen in the National League."*
— *Darryl Strawberry,*
Mets outfielder

DURING THE 1986 season, I
never had much of an opportunity to stop and think about what
was happening to me because I had to stay on such a careful day-
to-day program, so at the time I didn't really appreciate that I was
in the middle of a dream come true. First there was the twenty-
strikeout game, then we moved into first place, then the fourteen-
game winning streak. Then, not only did Dick Howser name me
to start the All-Star Game, but I was getting to start it the year
that it happened to be in my hometown. Back in March someone
had pointed out that the game was being played in Houston, and
I'd be lying if I tried to pretend that I didn't think or dream about
pitching in it.

There had been rumors for nearly a month that the Mets' ace
Dwight Gooden and I would be the starters, but it wasn't until the
previous Thursday—July 10th—that I knew it for certain, when
Howser named the pitchers. I started against California's Mike Witt
on the Saturday before the All-Star Game, and I was hoping that
it would be a somewhat easy game, so I could get out and get rested
since I knew I'd be starting in Houston on two days' rest. With Witt,
though, it had no chance of being easy. The Angels scored a run
off me in the fourth, and after we tied it they went ahead 2–1 in
the sixth on an error, a stolen base, and Wally Joyner's double. Buckner then hit a two-run homer in the bottom of the sixth, I held

on, broke the two-game losing streak, and was on my way home to Houston with a 15–2 record.

Needless to say, there was family everywhere in Katy and Houston. Anyone who was kin or cousin of any kind was showing up. There were six or seven television stations at the house on Monday, as well, and it was completely crazy. I finally told Deb and my mother that with the exception of Boston's Channel 38, which was taping a special, all the media people had to leave when my brother Richard and I left for the Astrodome and the workout. The rest of the time Richard and Randy played bodyguards.

When I got there, the atmosphere was a lot of fun. None of us had any idea that Howser was sick, for he didn't go for his tests until two days after the game. After he addressed the team, he called me into his office and talked for about twenty minutes. I knew what an exceptional person and manager he is, but what struck me was how much he wanted to win this game. I think a lot of American League players did, too. Maybe they were tired of always losing or being put down as the inferior league, but there was no question in the clubhouse that this was more than an exhibition. It was also neat for me because it was my first occasion to personally meet an Eddie Murray (Baltimore) or a Lance Parrish (Detroit) or a Wally Joyner (California). I'm their enemy, but we're all players and it was a great thrill to meet them and see them as people, not enemies. New York's Dave Winfield was a riot. He was telling funny stories about all the things that go on every day with the Yankees. He can talk just like George Steinbrenner, and he had everyone in stitches. "Now that I'm starting the All-Star Game," he asked a New York reporter, "can I play every day for the Yankees?" He was being platooned at the time, reportedly at Steinbrenner's request. Rice came up and said, "The only reason I'm here is to make sure that you have fun." Witt and I talked about all the times we'd battled each other over the season (little did we know that we'd meet again in the first game of the play-offs). Milwaukee's Ted Higuera and I became friends. But the guy I had the most fun with was Kirby Puckett from Minnesota. Our friendship had started in Toledo when I was playing for Pawtucket, and I told him we'd be going to the big leagues at the same time. He had a black glove. "Man, I gotta get me a black glove," I yelled at him. He kidded me about my throwing gas. I told him I'd throw him nothing but gas if he wouldn't swing from his heels. Sure enough, he tried to drag bunt, I threw him two sliders and a curveball, and we've been razzing each other ever since.

I was told that the pitchers weren't going to hit during the workout, but McNamara—whom Howser had picked as one of his coaches—came running in all excited, telling me I was supposed to be the first one in the cage. Puckett gave me one of his bats and a couple of batting gloves, and I took a few hacks, with Mac throwing to me. That was neat, too, with everyone watching my swing. I even took a few left-handed, and when I got out of there, Mac told someone he's glad that I don't have to hit during the regular season. Parrish and I went over some things in the outfield, and when the workout was over, I headed home for all the family. While I was there, Randy went over all the National League hitters with me.

To me, this game was a special opportunity. It was a chance not only to pitch against the guys in the other league, but a chance to prove that there can be dominating pitchers in the American League, too. We always hear all those clichés about the National being the fastball league and the American being the junkball league. Then, too, I knew that after the twenty-strikeout game and the fourteen-game winning streak, for me to be matched up with Gooden was something that people would want to watch (which they did, as ABC had record All-Star Game ratings). That made it a fan's game; we'd be watched and that made it all the more fun.

My family was all upset with some things former Baltimore pitcher Jim Palmer was quoted as saying in the Houston papers the morning of the game. They took all the quotes to mean that he thought I'd be hit hard and be out of there in the first two innings, which motivated me even further. As I've mentioned, it's almost always been a positive, motivating force for me when someone has said I couldn't do something, because I always take that "I'll-show-you" attitude. Palmer later told me that what he meant to say was that he'd pitched in five of these games, and knowing that there's a lot of adrenaline and excitement, he thought I might be apt to overthrow on two days' rest. Not only that, but with only two days' rest, I could have a little drop in my velocity. I loosened up and threw ten or fifteen pitches to Geddy the day before the game, and I told him, "I'll have to be a breaking ball pitcher; I don't have anything." My arm still felt heavy from Saturday's start, and that caused me not to sleep well.

However, when I woke up the day of the game, I felt great. I had a lot of anxiety, but I feel anxiety before every game I pitch, no matter if it's Opening Day, the World Series, or a Tuesday night in Cleveland with no one in the stands. I went out to warm up, threw two or three pitches, and I knew I had it. In addition, it was fun warming up, because the Dome makes the pop in the glove sound even louder than it really is. A hard thrower's warm-up sounds like a fireworks show, with every wham-wham-wham magnified two or three times; so I was just busting the ball as hard as I could into Geddy's glove.

The mound in the Dome is really nice, too. With a lot of mounds, when you rock back in your motion, it's hard to maintain your balance because the steepness isn't right. It's important to have it soft enough so that you can dig it out to push off, but not too sandy so it falls apart. I had thought that Dwight had a pretty long stride, but when I got out there, it turned out that we were landing in exactly the same hole. He throws from the left side of the mound, I guess because of his curveball. I move around; although, if I start a hitter in one spot, I'll stay there. At his next at bat, though, I'll change to give the hitter a different angle or look. The hitter will adjust from at bat to at bat, so I'll change from at bat to at bat also, because it is a game of constant adjustments. I'll move inches, although I've seen guys who move from side to side on every pitch or batter. But I don't feel it's where you start, but where you land your front foot. It's strange, but when you stand on some mounds, they seem very close to the plate, while others seem very far away. And the Dome mound seems very close. You get that feeling that you're right on top of the hitters.

I looked at the National League lineup and saw how much strength they had from top to bottom. However, any time a pitcher is facing a bunch of hitters for the first time, the pitcher has the advantage. So, since I figured I had the advantage on them, I decided the only thing to do was to go right after them and challenge them with my best heat.

Tony Gwynn of the Padres led off. My first thought about him was to remember that we had done a talk show together one Sunday night with commentator Bob Costas and that Gwynn had gone on about how glad he was that I was in the American League so he didn't have to face me. I knew he was a great contact hitter, a lot like Boggs. I also knew that he is a threat to steal any time he gets on, so I was conscious of getting ahead and throwing strikes. I guessed him to be a student, like Chicken Man, because when I peeked over at the National League bench as I was warming up, he was one guy who watched me closely. I threw him a good pitch, and even though it was caught, he still hit the ball pretty hard to left center. I had the jitters when I was facing him, but I felt as if my fastball was rising, and that's a confidence builder at any time. Whether or not the ball rises is one of those things that people argue about all the time, but I believe that my fastball does; I *know* I see it rise and take off.

Anyway, I was relieved to get the first out behind me. Then I struck out Ryne Sandberg of the Cubs with a fastball away that was probably my best pitch of the night. I got ahead, which enabled me to make my pitch—in this case, the fastball on the outside corner. It's so important for me to get ahead. We go over hitters with scouting reports in our meetings, and it seems that the scout writes "first pitch fastball hitter" about everyone that we face. Well, fastballs are the way I have to pitch, and I have to throw them for strikes early in the count; and once I get ahead, they have to hit my pitch. Sometimes there's a lot of backward thinking. Do they want me *not* to throw my best pitch and get ahead?

When I had gone down the NL lineup, I knew that Keith Hernandez of the Mets would be a tough out because he's such a good contact hitter. He was, too. He hit a good breaking ball to Joyner at first. I busted my tail to get to the bag, expecting a nice, soft toss similar to the ones I always get from Buckner, and Joyner threw me a pea.

That inning was almost it for me, due to a freak occurrence. I've broken my nose three times—once as a kid, once when the weight bench fell on me, once in football—and as a result, I've always had trouble with nosebleeds. I had a little cold and hadn't slept well the night before, so I went into the clubhouse after the first inning to blow my nose. Evidently, I blew it too hard, because when I did, it started bleeding badly. I started thinking that I was going to have to come out after one inning. Gene Monaghan and Bill Ziegler, the Yankees' and Rangers' trainers, came over and worked on me like a fighter between rounds. I'm surprised it didn't bleed later when I blew up in the Chicago game after being ejected on July 30, because sometimes when I get really excited or hyperventilate, it starts bleeding. I thought Monaghan and Ziegler were going to tell Howser to get me out of there, but they stopped it, and I took a napkin in the back of my pants to the on-deck circle.

Winfield hit a two-out double off Gooden in the bottom of the second. Dwight then got behind Detroit second baseman Lou Whitaker, and he hit it out, which made me immediately think, "There are my two runs." He came across the plate, Winfield shook his hand, and when I grabbed him, I said, "Why'd you have to do it with me on deck? Dwight'll be mad." I had Marty Barrett's bat, the lightest one I could find to bring with me. I actually didn't get too bad a swing at the first pitch. But I was so late, I hit it between the first base coaching box and the National League dugout. I looked over and said to them, "Either get down or get a glove." The next pitch was a fastball on the outside corner for a called strike. Now, I thought it was outside, but only because he threw it so hard that it looked like a long way out there. The third pitch started for my neck; I started to bail and then realized "Oh, no, it's a curveball," and tried to get back in there as it got to Gary Carter's glove so it appeared that I was on the pitch like a real hitter. Which I wasn't, of course. When I saw Gooden downstairs afterward, I told him he was cheating.

Hitting against Gooden was good for me, because it reiterated how important the fastball is. He was being clocked anywhere from 90 to 93 mph, and it seemed as if it was getting in on me in a hurry. At times in the second half of the season, when I started losing confidence in my fastball, I'd think back to hitting against Dwight and remember how quickly a hitter has to make up his mind and how a good fastball can make the strike zone seem much bigger than it appears from the mound. It's a psychological game, and you've got to use everything that you've got.

When I went back out for the bottom of the second, it was much easier to go right after hitters, especially with Parrish catching. He and Gedman are both great to throw to because they've got such broad shoulders, and I like to use shoulder points and knee points and throw off them; I try to break Geddy's kneecap every time I go down and away, and I was able to do the same thing with Parrish. Carter popped up to lead off the inning; then up came Darryl Strawberry of the Mets. When Randy and I went over the hitters the day before, we were talking about how Strawberry had hit the speaker in dead center field in the home run hitting contest. From what

I saw, however, he held the bat very high—he had it wrapped around his head and had to take a long swing—so there was no way that I was going to throw him any kind of off-speed pitch. I told Parrish that I refused to give this guy any kind of a chance, because he can hit the breaking ball *out* out of the Dome. I thought that as long as I keep the fastball where I want it and keep it off Broadway, I'd be all right. I did, and he struck out. Mike Schmidt (of Philadelphia) hit his ball very well, but in the Dome it was just an out.

As I walked off the mound at the end of that inning, I was thinking that it sure is a different way to make a living pitching in the Dome as opposed to Fenway. I take nothing away from anyone in the National League, but when Tudor came back to see his old Red Sox teammates in the clubhouse this spring, he was saying how many more good pitchers' parks there are in the National League than there are in the American. In the American, most of them are home run parks, and even three of the four artificial turf stadiums—Toronto, Minnesota, Seattle—are bandboxes. If you go to Detroit, all you face are left-handers. I read that when Whitey Herzog offered four pitchers (Joaquin Andujar, Ricky Horton, Jeff Lahti, Kurt Kepshire) for Hurst, he said that he liked to look at where a young pitcher learned to pitch. That's one reason he went after Tudor. It's a lot easier when you go from a small to a large park than if you learned to pitch in a St. Louis, then got traded to the Red Sox. You have to learn to live with home runs you can't believe are possible. I remember one time I threw a 2–2 pitch that broke Dave Kingman's bat. He was jogging down to first, thinking it was a routine out. The wind wasn't even blowing out that much. I looked up, Jimmy was standing there, I started to walk off, and the ball hit the top of the wall and went into the net. You have to maintain your concentration level in Fenway, whereas in some of those big parks, you can make a pretty bad mistake and walk off the mound with a routine out.

In my third inning, I got three ground balls. Atlanta's Dale Murphy hit a ball hard into the shortstop hole, and Cal Ripken of the Orioles made a good play on it. Ozzie Smith of St. Louis and pinch hitter Randy Bass of the Astros both grounded to Whitaker at second, and I was out of there with nine up and nine down. I went up into the clubhouse to ice my arm, do my shoulder exercises, and begin to prepare for my Saturday start in Seattle, and I heard the television announcers talking about how I'd hit 97 or 98 on the gun, that I was the sixth American Leaguer to retire nine straight batters, and that twenty-one of my twenty-five pitches were strikes.

Around the seventh, some guy came in and told me that if the 3–0 lead held up, I was going to be the MVP, so I stayed around and had to watch poor Geddy. He had no way to catch Texas's Charlie Hough's knuckler, especially with the glove they gave him. He had one of those oversize gloves, which he'd never used, and to make it worse, it belonged to backup Texas catcher Orlando Mercado,

THE ALL-STAR GAME: JULY 15, 1986

AL, 3–2

AMERICAN	ab	r	h	bi	NATIONAL	ab	r	h	bi
Puckett cf	3	0	1	0	Gwynn lf	3	0	0	0
Henderson lf	3	0	0	0	Sax 2b	1	0	1	1
Moseby lf	0	0	0	0	Sandberg 2b	3	0	0	0
Boggs 3b	3	0	1	0	Scott p	0	0	0	0
Jacoby 3b	1	0	0	0	S.Fernandez p	0	0	0	0
Parrish c	3	0	0	0	G.Davis ph	1	0	0	0
Rice ph	1	0	0	0	Krukow p	0	0	0	0
Gedman c	0	0	0	0	Hernandez 1b	4	0	0	0
Joyner 1b	1	0	0	0	Carter c	3	0	0	0
Mattingly 1b	3	0	0	0	J.Davis c	1	0	1	0
Ripken ss	4	0	0	0	Pena pr	0	0	0	0
T.Frnandz ss	0	0	0	0	Strawbrry rf	2	0	1	0
Winfield rf	1	1	1	0	Parker rf	2	0	1	0
Barfield rf	3	0	0	0	Schmidt 3b	1	0	0	0
Whitaker 2b	2	1	1	2	Brown 3b	2	1	1	0
White 2b	2	1	1	1	Murphy cf	2	0	0	0
Clemens p	1	0	0	0	C.Davis cf	1	0	0	0
Higuera p	1	0	0	0	O. Smith ss	1	0	0	0
Baines ph	1	0	0	0	Brooks ss	2	1	0	0
Hough p	0	0	0	0	Gooden p	0	0	0	0
Righetti p	0	0	0	0	Bass ph	1	0	0	0
Aase p	0	0	0	0	Valenzuela p	0	0	0	0
					Rains lf	2	0	0	0
Totals	**33**	**3**	**5**	**3**	**Totals**	**32**	**2**	**5**	**1**

American   020 000 100–3
National   000 000 020–2

Game Winning RBI—Whitaker.

E—Sandberg. DP—American 1. LOB—American 5, National 4. 2B—Winfield, Brown. HR—Whitaker, White. SB—Puckett, Moseby, Sax.

	IP	H	R	ER	BB	SO
American						
Clemens W, 1-0	3	0	0	0	0	2
Higuera	3	1	0	0	1	2
Hough	1⅔	2	2	1	0	3
Righetti	0⅔	2	0	0	0	0
Aase S, 1	0⅔	0	0	0	0	0
National						
Gooden L, 0-1	3	3	2	2	0	2
Valenzuela	3	1	0	0	0	5
Scott	1	1	1	1	0	2
Fernandez	1	0	0	0	2	3
Krukow	1	0	0	0	0	0

Wild pitch—Hough. Balk—Gooden, Hough. Passed ball—Gedman. Umpires —Home, Froemming (NL); First, Palermo (AL); Second, Runge (NL); Third, Reed (AL); Left, Gregg (NL); Right, McClelland (AL). T—2:28. A—45,774.

and it was so new and stiff that Geddy couldn't close on the ball. Oh well, we held on and won 3–2, I got the MVP [Carl Yastrzemski is the only other Red Sox player to have won that award, which he earned with his four hits in the 1970 game], and again I was a little surprised because everyone in the clubhouse was as happy as if we were the Red Sox and we'd just finished a sweep of the Yankees or Tigers. Hough had a few problems because of Gedman's glove, but Higuera, Righetti, and Don Aase (of Baltimore) were all super as well. I guess there are some hard throwers in our league, after all.

My family had a little hoedown get-together that night, and the next day we had a picnic and barbecue and relaxed. We've all got egos, and after pitching against such great players, it was fun to read what some of them had to say about me in the papers. Gooden said, "I thought it was fun just to sit in the dugout and watch another power pitcher like him." Strawberry said, "No one in the National League throws as hard as he does." Gwynn was quoted as saying that Gooden and I are "in a class by themselves" and "what impressed me was that he can take something off both his fastball and curveball and hit spots." Schmidt said, "He's everything I expected. What makes him different is his slider, which makes him especially tough on right-handed batters. If Gooden threw a slider, I'd have retired long ago." Reading those things gave me a thrill, but when I got on the plane on Thursday night and headed for Seattle, I forgot about all the words. I also tried to leave my 15–2 record behind in the Boston clubhouse. I realized that things had gone beyond my wildest dreams, with the twenty strikeouts and the fourteen-game streak, and now the All-Star MVP Award. But they were past, and if I wanted to make this a truly extraordinary season, I'd have to forget the 15–2 and go out and try to pitch just as well in the second half. What was really important was getting into the play-offs. Opportunities like these simply don't happen every year.

When I got to Seattle for the beginning of the second half of the season on July 17, it had started to get quiet in the clubhouse. Even Fish was quiet, and he almost always is chirping. I guess he understood that some players might take chatter the wrong way.

Nip was still struggling to get his arm back into shape after rushing himself back on June 25, and he still felt as if just lifting his arm was a weighty effort. Hurst hadn't started since May, and while he was due to return on July 21, he and everyone knew that it would take a few starts to regain the sharpness and confidence he had when he pulled his groin. Sammy Stewart was still hurt. And, of course, none of us knew where Oil Can was.

The problems with Can had started back on the day the all-star pitchers were named. The American League had already named its starting players, so that day of July 10 at Fenway, we were waiting for a six P.M. announcement of whom Howser and the league officials had selected for our eight-man pitching staff. I pretty much knew I was going to be selected; Howser had already named me the starter. Now, Can deserved to make the team, just as he'd deserved to make it in 1985 when Sparky Anderson left him off. Can was second to me in wins (11–5), he'd been sensational in May, beaten the Yankees in the big game in New York, and was on his way to a possible twenty-win season. But there had been speculation in the papers that he wouldn't make it for two reasons: every team has to be represented, which means some players who ordinarily wouldn't be chosen have to be selected, and he was scheduled to start on the Sunday before the Tuesday All-Star Game. The league had reportedly decreed that anyone who starts on Sunday couldn't be chosen, which was one of the reasons Can didn't make it last year, either. We all hoped that Can would make it, because we knew that he'd get very upset if he didn't, and we knew we needed him in the second half. Nip kept saying, "I hope he makes it." I suggested that since I'd trade a pennant for some individual honor, if they could only take one of us I almost wish they'd pick Oil Can and have me stay home.

All the television stations had live units set up to interview us, and somewhere around six the official word came. Can, who isn't known for being at the park early, was there at four because he was so excited about being picked. I was inside the clubhouse, but I heard that a reporter broke the news to him that once again he'd been bypassed. I wasn't watching, but apparently he came into the clubhouse and was very upset. Now, I didn't know whether he had a $25,000 incentive for making the team or whether he needed the money. I don't know all the other problems that he had, be they financial, family, or whatever. But a lot of players have serious personal problems, and they can't put them ahead of the team. It's tough sometimes. Barrett got booed heavily for leaving some run-ners on base in a couple of games in August, but his son had had a bad bicycle accident at home, had been taken to the hospital, and it shook Marty up. He said nothing and snapped right out of it after two games. Look how Boggs came back from the tragic death of his mother. Look how Gedman played through the death of his father and stepsister. I know McNamara told Haywood Sullivan and Lou Gorman not to put any All-Star Game incentives in Boyd's 1987 contract. Mac has to pick the team. I hope he picks Can.

Boyd's locker is right inside the door as you come up from the runway and is across the clubhouse from me, and since I was get-ting changed I didn't see much. I *heard* a few things, but I tried to mind my business. I read where he tore off his uniform, which upset McNamara. Then Can began cursing. I'm sure he didn't even know what he was saying, but when he started cursing Nip and Fischer, it upset me and badly hurt them. Can and Nip had been friends for years, and Fish had constantly worked hard with him. Even if they weren't close, Nip is his teammate, Fischer his coach, and they are people with whom he worked and played; teammates play behind you or work with you and stand behind you. Some-times when Fish goes out to talk to Can, Can's so upset that he doesn't hear his coach, and Fischer never loses patience. He also protected him carefully. In June, Can wasn't throwing so well, and Fish kept telling people—especially the media—that he was throwing 90–91. I asked Ace Adams, our batting practice pitcher who ran the radar gun, if he weren't closer to 85, and Ace said,

"You're still not even close." Then, maybe worst of all, Can ended up screaming at Dr. Pappas and McNamara. That was really bad, for McNamara had done things for Can that the public never understood, and Dr. Pappas probably ended up helping him as much as anyone.

We players did know that Can was very emotional. We didn't know until he returned weeks later and read some of the stories that he apparently had some problems with tantrums that he admitted. We all hope that he's working things out; he's a terrific person whom I like very much. Can also *is* an all-star, a great pitcher. He's just emotional. He's got to pitch, and when he pitches he has to be high-strung. That's the way he concentrates and operates. He fires himself up from hitter to hitter. But it was hard for us to accept letting personal setbacks interfere with the team, especially in this season when the attitude of the Red Sox had turned 180 degrees. Can had walked out the year before, too. He'd lost a tough game to the Texas Rangers and all of a sudden started yelling in the shower about not getting runs. He was screaming at the top of his lungs, and finally as he came out of the shower, Rice went up to him and told him to be quiet. They had their confrontation, and Can didn't come to the park the next day.

The thing I learned early in life is that the team is the most important thing. Teammates may make errors, but they're not trying to make errors. Look, there is essential selfishness in the game. There has to be. It's an individual sport to some degree, you have to do your job no matter what, and you get paid for what you do as an individual (look what happened to Geddy after we won when he went to do his contract!). If a hitter goes four for four and we lose, he isn't necessarily happy, but he knows he did his job. He just can't *show* how he feels. It's possible to be selfish, but not jealous. You've got to want to be better than the next guy, but in friendly competition without the jealousy. The Red Sox weren't entirely that way the past year, so what we had going in 1986 was especially important not to mess up.

Anyway, Can threw down his uniform—which upset Mac, who said he "desecrated" it—and left. He later claimed that he tried to come back to the clubhouse and apologize, but Mac had told the clubhouse attendant to keep him out. All we knew then was what was in the papers, and the papers were filled with Can (he made the front page of the *Herald* eight times in thirteen days). We saw the picture of him throwing a soft drink at a cameraman. There were all sorts of rumors. At that point, when he hadn't come to the park either Friday or Saturday, he had to come back and show that personal things wouldn't get in the way of the team. He came back, and, with tears in his eyes, apologized and told us how badly he wanted us to forgive him. But as Baylor said, "He has to prove himself by action, not words. Words don't mean a thing in this game."

Then the day after the All-Star Game, the story came out that Can got grabbed by some police in Chelsea. When I was flying to Seattle, I read that he'd come to the park, hadn't rejoined the team, and was going to the hospital in Worcester for some sort of tests. We the players still didn't know what was going on, and when we heard about the police incident, we figured he was really in some sort of trouble. We didn't know; all we were doing was speculating. And hoping that he was all right.

The stretch after the All-Star break is still the most pressure that I've ever endured. With so many of the other starters out or in rehabilitation, Seaver not getting any wins, and a lot of regular players hurting, I kept hearing teammates say, "Don't worry, Rocket's going tomorrow." Don't get me wrong, I like pressure. I wouldn't like pitching so much if I didn't thrive on it. I always wanted to pitch because I'm either the hero or I'm the dog, I get the win or I get the loss. I like the attention; I figure that's the Reggie in me. We won three out of thirteen games in the stretch from the Witt game on July 12 to Chicago on July 28, and all three wins happened to be mine. But at the time, I was more bothered by what we thought was everyone waiting for us to fold. Most of the players on this team weren't part of the past. What did I know about 1978? About the only players that were around in the past were Evans, Stanley, and Rice; and Rice and Evans weren't talking about what might or might not happen to us. Most of us didn't understand why everyone was so concerned with the past, and some of the guys who read the papers every day got pretty upset about it. I figured that we'd already withstood the challenges of the Yankees and Orioles, and we'd already withstood the loss of Nipper and Hurst. We'd get our rotation back healthy by the first of August and play the last two months the way we did the first two.

But there was a lot of pressure at that point because of all the public concern about our "choke," so after we lost the first two games of the Seattle series 5–1 (on Presley's eleventh-inning grand slam off Stanley) and 10–4, I was glad to get three first-inning runs in my start so we could all relax and I could go to work. Getting those runs early is what momentum is all about, which is why it's so important for a pitcher at home to set down the side in the first. It helps a visiting pitcher when he begins with an advantage.

We had a little incident in that game on July 19. There were a couple of Mariners who were trying to take me way back to the upper deck, trying to hit a hole in the Dome. Alvin Davis had homered off me earlier, and when he came up in the seventh, Geddy said something to him and he said something back. Then when I struck him out, Geddy had to pick up the ball and throw to first, so Davis had to run down there. I yelled something to Buckner, and Davis thought I was talking to him and yelled something. Geddy then said something else, and I added, "That's what they get for trying to hit it out of the country." There was some milling around and people had to be separated. Hey, Davis is a great guy, and he was probably frustrated. I can understand. When teams are losing, the players look at everything completely different, and the Mariners probably feel that other teams try to rub it in. When Henderson and Owen joined us, Baylor said, "Welcome to the big leagues." They nodded, too. (When we were in Seattle, McNamara called me into his office and asked me about Spike. He wanted to know what kind of person he was and whether he'd fit into our program, so when we were at a UT function, I told Spike that I thought he was coming over to us in a trade.)

We lost three out of four in Seattle. Then we went on to Oakland and hit bottom. Rice was hurt. We were platooning LaSchelle Tarver and Kevin Romine in center, Mike Stenhouse was at first, and Baylor even had to play left because of all the other injuries. The A's beat us three straight. Hurst returned to start the first game and pitched well despite losing 5–2. He obviously wasn't close to his peak form in one start. He had to go out and build up to the point where he could air it out and not worry about re-injuring his groin and/or damaging his arm. Those are difficult hurdles. Seaver then lost another tough game, Nip had a rough outing, and we headed for Anaheim with our lead back down to three games.

I had that Friday night, the 25th, against John Candelaria, who had pitched very well against us July 13 in Boston. We were 1–6 on the trip, we'd lost four in a row for the first time all season, and had dropped eight of ten. There were 51,000 there in Anaheim Stadium, but it turned out to be fun. Buckner knocked in two runs in the third off Candelaria, and then Geddy put it out of hand with a grand slam off Vern Ruhle in the fifth. At that time, I still had a no-hitter, which I lost in the bottom of the fifth when Reggie hit an opposite field double and scored. After the game, Buckner told the reporters that when I'm on the mound, "we all have the feeling we're going to win, so we relax and hit better." [When the Red Sox were 3–10 after the All-Star break, they scored seventeen runs in Clemens' three starts and seventeen runs in the other ten games.] Reggie was quoted in the papers as saying I'm in the "Twilight Zone." That made me laugh.

When Witt and Don Sutton beat Hurst and Seaver 4–1 and 3–0 in our last two West Coast games and we headed to Chicago with a three-game lead, all of New England worried that we were going to fold. Seaver shrugged it off, and the younger players listened to him. "You can't go through a season without a down period, no matter how good a team you have," he said. "We're a good team, and we will start winning again. Soon."

How right he was, as usual. Nip started the next night in Chicago. In the five starts after he came back against the Yankees, his arm simply hadn't bounced back, and I'm certain his legs hadn't either. He had a terrible earned run average (8.04) in those starts, but when we had to have a victory and still weren't hitting, he came up with a crucial 3–1 seven-hitter. As it turned out, that was especially important, because I was about to go into my second two-game losing streak, which started on one of the strangest plays I've ever been involved in.

On July 30, we were in the bottom of the fifth inning, and the White Sox had rallied for two runs to tie it at 2–2. There were two outs with a runner on third when Harold Baines hit a ground ball to Buckner. He made a lob-ball of a toss to me, so I wanted to make sure the first base umpire, Greg Kosc, knew that I had the ball when my foot was on the bag. But before I even got to the bag, I looked at Kosc and he already had his arms out to call Baines safe. It was crazy. You could hear the spikes on the bag. I left my foot behind like I missed it, and maybe that fooled him, but I didn't want him to think I pulled my foot off. I turned around, bent over, and marked the spot where there was one Puma imprint pointing toward the crowd and everybody else's pointing toward home plate. Between halves of the inning, the ground crew had dragged the infield, so the marks were clear; ten minutes later, Stapleton came out and pointed to the same thing to show the crew chief, Richie Garcia.

"You missed it," hollered Kosc. "I stepped right on it, here it is," I yelled back at him, and stood up. I was leaning toward him as I came up, but he was leaning toward me, too. That's what caused the contact. But it was his forearm that touched me for the initial contact. Then, when I was getting up, I was over his leg. That's when he threw me out, and I couldn't believe it. Now, Buckner and Kosc had gotten into it pretty badly in Seattle in May, and Buck was finally ejected after a pretty ugly scene. I think that may have had some carryover. Kosc also later said that I swore at him, but I didn't until he threw me out. It's just lucky I was so angry that I'd forgotten that the go-ahead run had scored because he missed the call [it was the winning run in the final 7–2 outcome, which was one of Clemens' four losses].

In all the argument that raged on, I hyperventilated twice. One time I started getting black in my eyes, so Mac took over the argument. I took two deep breaths and resumed my hollering. Barrett, Hurst, and Nipper all got into it, too, and finally Baylor grabbed me. At first he didn't realize how angry I was and didn't have a strong enough grip on me, so I broke loose. Then he put a clamp on me a truck couldn't have escaped. Rice then grabbed my other leg and they hauled me off the field. "We can't afford to get you suspended, and if you keep this up you'll be in big trouble," Rice said to me. When I yelled something else at Kosc, Rice got stern. "Get in the clubhouse right now and shut up, we can't afford to lose you." Nipper got thrown out and yelled, "Forty-five thousand people didn't come to see you umpire." Even Hurst got ejected. They each got fined $100 for "prolonging the incident," and I paid their fines. One umpire reported that Hurst had used profanity, which is one of the most ridiculous things I've ever heard. He *might* have yelled "gosh darn." (The closest he ever came to swearing was before I got to the big leagues. He was frustrated, he felt that the manager and coaches were making unfair character judgments about him, and one night he and Johnny Pesky got into it in the food line in Cleveland. Hurst called Pesky a name—hardly a bad cussword—and Tom Burgmeier said, "There goes a chip out of the monument in Salt Lake City.") As it turned out, all I lost was a day's pay—

little more than $1000—and $2.50. I got a two-game suspension, but it was for a doubleheader August 12 in Kansas City. I went to the park that day, worked from 12:30 to 2:30, stayed around in my long underwear, did my arm weights, and watched the game on TV.

Getting ejected had been a tough night for me, but I think some good eventually came of it. For the team, it was but another one of those pegs in the big pegboard, like the twenty-strikeout game. We really pulled back together as a team. It was a tremendous feeling to know that my teammates would stand up behind me so strongly. To see Stape and Marty and everyone standing with me was important, and after a rough three-week stretch, we needed something to get us fired back up. I learned something else, too, in this case about umpires. Soon thereafter we had the Garcia-Kosc crew in Boston. Greg came up and said, "No hard feelings?" He meant it, too. The umpires have a job to do, too, and these things will happen. I had Garcia behind the plate on September 5 against the Twins, and it was as if nothing had happened. [Of Clemens' ninety-seven pitches that night, Garcia called but twenty-nine balls, less than 29 percent.]

After that, things began coming back together. Hurst was getting better and better. We'd heard that Oil Can was finishing his treatment in the hospital, was gaining weight, and getting ready to return with the blessing of the club and Dr. Pappas, who may have saved his life. Rice had gotten his agent, George Kalafatis, to take over Can's affairs and try to straighten out his money problems, and it appeared that he was going to be able to help us down the stretch. We got home and won two out of three from the Royals to get the lead back up to 4½, and I was pretty excited about going for my eighteenth win on August 4 (my twenty-fourth birthday) on national television.

It's strange how these things go. Here I've gone through a fourteen-game winning streak and went into two starts in six days against Chicago with a 17–2 record. In both games I face a guy (Jose DeLeon) who was 2–19 the year before. And he wins both games, my last two losses of the season. Now, DeLeon has great stuff. Anyone who sees him knows that. He was very tough in this Fenway game, allowing only two hits and retiring twelve straight at one point. But I had a shutout into the eighth as well. Although Dr. Pappas said, "This is the day you're supposed to get all the gifts," it didn't exactly work out that way. The seventh started when Carlton Fisk hit a ball that took a funny hop off Boggs' chest, which was scored an error. But I was the one who messed things up. Ozzie Guillen laid down a quick drag bunt along the first base line. He'd shown it the first time, so Buck was charging on the first pitch. I'd already busted down the line. I had two problems: I grabbed a handful of grass and then had to throw between Buck and the runner. I threw a high change-up that sailed out of my hand. If Kevin McHale had been playing first, I'd have been all right, but Marty isn't Kevin McHale. The ball ended up in right, and I had a runner on first. To make things worse, Julio Cruz got the run in with a sacrifice fly on an 0–2 pitch. When I got Cruz 0 and 2, I was thinking about showing him a breaking ball, but I figured that at that stage of the game, if I'm going to get beaten, I'm going to get beaten on my best pitch. I tried to waste a good fastball up out of the strike zone, he got around on it, and he knocked it into center field.

My outlook was that two tough losses like that come with the territory, like an 8–5 win in California when you don't necessarily deserve to win. In three of my losses, we'd scored a total of four runs, but you know that's going to happen over the year. It's like a hard candy Christmas. You have to plan on those things to retain your balance, like bad hops. But all of a sudden I started getting questions like, "You're three and four since the streak ended—are you concerned?" There was speculation that my arm was tired. Which it wasn't. I think veterans like Baylor, Sambito, and Seaver were most bothered by all the worry about us folding and my losing and all that stuff.

The team hitting slump continued the next night, August 5, when Can made his return and lost 3–1 to a three-hitter by Chicago's Richard Dotson. But the game was encouraging just for Can's strong performance. We all read some of what he'd gone through in *Sports Illustrated*, Baylor talked at length to Dr. Pappas, and a reporter close to Boyd had told players they should keep an open mind. "You'll be fine if you stick to what you do so well," I told Boyd, "and that is pitch. Remember Winter Haven. Remember the pledge we pitchers made to one another. Remember that we now have Tom Seaver. Let's get together and win this thing."

We had had one important psychological boost back on August 3 against Kansas City. That was the first time Mac gave Calvin the opportunity to close out a game. We were ahead 5–3 in the ninth when Nip gave up two hits. Calvin came in and struck out Frank White, blew away Steve Balboni, and got Mike Kingery to ground out. The fans had a new hero, chanting, "Cal-*Vin*, Cal-*Vin*," and I think it boosted everyone. There's something about having that big hard-thrower coming out of the pen that gives a team confidence. Not that our bull pen had been that bad, because they'd done a good job and were near the top of the league in saves. But Mac may have lost some confidence, and the fans certainly had. (Stanley worried all the time about the fans and what was in the paper [his ERA for the season was 6.00 in Fenway, 2.91 on the road]. He switched his locker to the one that Torrez and Eckersley had had. He said he liked Fenway better without fans. He didn't need to worry so much. He's too good a pitcher.) Calvin could be a great reliever, with 91–94 mile per hour gas and a low-key personality. He's best if he's used for a maximum of four, five, or six outs, but after the season he was being convinced that he should take up a weights program similar to mine. He had some shoulder breakdown, so it just wasn't as strong as it used to be. He told me in December that he's starting to try to do what I do to build and maintain the shoulder muscles.

Even with Calvin's boost, we were still having trouble scoring runs. After the August 5 loss, McNamara made an important decision. He decided to change the lineup, put Boggs in the leadoff spot and Barrett to the second position—and it worked. The Orioles at that point had snuck within 2½ games, and the Tigers—whom many had picked because of their pitching—were creeping up and were four games out. We knew we had to play them seven times from August 8 to August 17. The lineup switch certainly worked. We scored nine runs against Chicago on August 6, and Hurst showed he was all the way back with a shutout. We headed for Detroit with a 9–0 victory.

Boggs, however, wasn't too happy about the lineup change. He had lost his arbitration case the previous February when they said he didn't drive in enough runs, but he sure made an impact in the leadoff spot. He was on base fourteen of the first seventeen times he came up and batted .389 the remainder of the season to finish at .357. [Boggs' .352 career average is eighth all-time for players after five full major league seasons.]

The August 8–11 series was Detroit's run at us, just the way the Yankees and Orioles had had their runs in June. Media from all around the country came in, and the Detroit papers were filled with their charge. But Sparky Anderson made a strange decision, given the importance of the series. He started Jack Morris, his ace, in Cleveland the night before, and decided to use Randy O'Neal, who was 1–6, to start against us. O'Neal turned out to be very wild. We got four runs on one hit in the second, and that was all Seaver needed. He pitched an absolute masterpiece, a five-hit, 6–1 win, in which he went from the first to the sixth without allowing a hit. That certainly was one of the turning point games of the season, like the opener in New York. Nip and Schiraldi won 8–7 the next night, and then we won my start on Sunday, August 10. Not that I got the win, because I left in the seventh with a 3–2 lead. Darrell Evans hit a grand slam off Tim Lollar. Then Geddy pinch-hit a grand slam off Willie Hernandez—the second homer he'd ever hit off a lefty and the second homer Hernandez had allowed to a left-handed batter in three years—to win it 9–6. When Mac told Gedman to pinch-hit, everyone on the bench was asking, "What's going on?" Then he got a hanging breaking ball up in his eyes, toma-hawked it, and it ended up in the second row of the lower deck.

I was throwing the ball really well early that day, but it was tough weather to pitch in. When I warmed up, it was hot and muggy, so I took off my sweatshirt. However, by the third inning, it was raining hard—a cold rain. Alan Trammell one-handed a little slider out of the park, which didn't bother me, but it got muddier and muddier, and by the sixth inning, I was having trouble getting my balance. That sort of stuff is tough on a power pitcher, because it becomes practically impossible to have a strong leg drive. Sparky came out in the fifth and tried to stall, waiting for the rain, and he got me keyed. He kept coming out and trying to stall me. That doesn't work with me. Coaches were hollering at me as a rookie, and I think it's funny. Sparky came out and was complaining about something I was doing. Marty came in to the mound. Sparky was in the middle of the umpires. I said something like "let's go," and he got hot. He was looking at the umpires but he was talking to me when he said, "Don't you ever say anything or butt into one of my conversations, young man." Marty looked over. "Let's go," he yelled at Sparky, and I think he thought it was me. So—what the heck—I yelled, "This ain't working," and one of the umps came and pulled me away. I like to see managers and umpires arguing, but not that afternoon. It was cold and wet and I was stiffening up.

That was also a game I'll never forget for one pitch. When I came in after the third inning, Nip was talking to someone about the gun readings. It was the tough gun, too, the Ray Gun (which judges the speed of the ball when it crosses the plate and is both slower and more accurate than the JUGGS gun, which judges the speed as it leaves the pitcher's hand). "Do you think you're throwing hard?" Nip asked. "Well, you just broke the sound barrier. You threw a ball to Gibson at one hundred miles an hour." I immediately knew which pitch it was, and I really didn't try to throw it hard. I just got the ball out in front of me and let it go and everything was right there. It was just the way it's supposed to be in front of the mirror. It was thrown to Gibson, and I was thinking about what a quick bat he has; I kept seeing that ball he hit off Rich Gossage in the 1984 World Series into the upper deck. If I looked at a film of that 100 mph pitch, I know it would look as if I didn't even throw the ball. Sometimes when I'm throwing my hardest, I'll look at the film and it appears that I'm not even trying. Then when I grunt and hump up, I may throw 88. We were four months into the season and I was getting stronger.

We'd responded to the Detroit challenge by winning three straight in their ballpark, and when the seven-game, two-weekend series against them was over, we'd won five and Morris had won two. Sparky ended up rushing Morris back on three days' rest to pitch the fourth game in Detroit, so I wonder if he lost any sleep on the decision not to hold him back to oppose Seaver.

I beat the Tigers 8–5 the following Friday, August 15, in Fenway, although I didn't pitch too well. The mechanics that had started to get messed up in the rain in Detroit carried over, and Sambito came in to get his eleventh save. People may not appreciate the job Sambito did over the season, but when he was being used to get left-handers or close out games, he had a heck of a season. Left-handed batters hit only .184 against him, and he prevented 78.2 percent of inherited runners from scoring [best on the team, followed by Schiraldi's 72.7 percent, Stanley's 65.5 percent, and Stewart's 52.2 percent]. It wasn't until my next start, in Minnesota August 20, that I began to get my form and timing back. I walked six and threw two wild pitches in that 9–1 win in the Metrodome, but I threw a two-hitter. Not only that, but I didn't give up a gopher ball. That in itself was an accomplishment.

We made the deal for Owen and Henderson from Seattle our first night in Minnesota. They were both excited to go from last to first place, but that night there was a holdup (Gorman didn't realize that he needed waivers on Mike Brown and Mike Trujillo since they were in AAA), and they were worried they might be sent back. The first person we introduced Spike to was Stanley, since they weren't exactly on the best of terms. That first night Spike, Calvin, and I sat in the clubhouse almost the entire game talking about old times. Spike was perfect for us. He's a vacuum, he's good on turf, and he's so good an infielder that when you've got two outs and the ball is hit to him, you start walking off the field. Spike is never too high, never too low, but he's always smiling, always has energy, is always trying to pick people up. That whole week I was telling people we should trade for Jim Acker, Keith Moreland, Capel, Bruce Ruffin, Brumley . . . and hire Gus as the third base coach. It was great, just as it had been the previous fall when Cal and I were driving to Jackson, Mississippi, for his wedding and I told him that I heard that we were getting him from the Mets. The one thing that surprised me about the Owen deal is who we gave up: Rey Quinones. Ted Williams said he was the best player the Red Sox had developed in twenty years, and Gorman called him a surefire Hall of Famer. Nevertheless, I can't speculate on what would have happened had we had someone else at short. But I do know this: the Red Sox won with Spike Owen at shortstop. He turned out to be the vacuum, and he and Barrett turned the double play as well as anyone in the league. Don't think the pitchers didn't appreciate that down the stretch.

That August 20 game was my nineteenth victory, so I was heading home to Texas to try and win number twenty. It couldn't have been nearer to being perfect. All my family and friends were there. Deb had gone home early to get everyone up there. Not only that, but she bought me a present for good luck. She does that a lot, but usually it's a polo shirt, or something like that. But when I opened the door to my hotel room, there was this little dog running around. It was three inches by three inches and was called Gizmo. I couldn't believe it. (It turned out to be funny, though, because Jack Rogers let me take Gizmo home on the plane. The dog could go on the charter, but Deb couldn't.)

On that day, August 25, the setting seemed perfect. I had on my "United States of Texas" T-shirt, which George Bush liked so much at the All-Star Game. Previously, I'd gone into the eighth inning with a no-hitter here and had won the All-Star Game across the state. It was my favorite hot, muggy weather, and I knew I had good stuff. I took a two-hitter into the eighth and had a 2–0 lead over Bobby Witt—the Canton, Massachusetts, kid from the University of Oklahoma whom Danny Doyle compared to me. With one out in the eighth, Ruben Sierra beat out an infield hit, and with two out, up came a pinch hitter named Gene Petralli.

To be honest, I'd never heard of the guy. I called Geddy out, but he didn't know anything about him either. He looked into the dugout, but we didn't have anything in Lach's books or charts. We decided to just go after him. I looked at him and he was about five-foot-eight; he was choked halfway up the bat and looked like all he was going to do was slap the ball on the ground and run like a rabbit. I let go with a fastball. It ran right back over the plate a little, he bailed, and he hit it over the right field fence. I couldn't believe it. Calvin gave up a homer to Sierra—no disgrace, because he's one of the best young players in the game—in the tenth, and we lost.

The next afternoon, while we were shagging in the outfield, Seaver and I got into a little discussion. He asked me some questions, and finally he asked, "What were you thinking when you threw that pitch?" I told him the whole business about Petralli's looking like a rabbit.

"But you didn't *know*, did you?" Seaver replied. He proceeded to tell me that if he had my fastball, he'd have wasted a ball up and away, one he never could have pulled. "That way you could get a look at what he was trying to do by his reaction," said Seaver. "Even with good hitters I know well, if I'm in a situation, I'll waste a pitch to watch his first move with his hands or feet and figure out what he's trying to do." Tom Seaver taught me a lesson I'll never forget.

Seaver didn't come over and lecture other pitchers; he wouldn't say much unless you asked him. The first week he asked me about my slider, and made a suggestion on the grip. He talked about situations, and about leg drive and how when Mac comes out to ask us how we feel, we always respond in terms of our legs, not our shoulders. The other time he helped me immensely was later, during the World Series before the sixth game, where he knew that I was exactly two inches off in my leg lift and made suggestions to cope with both the mound and the atmosphere in New York at a time when I needed it most. Tom and Nip were already friends, and Nip was always asking him questions. Whenever I asked Tom about my delivery, he'd say, "Don't ask me anything, it's perfect." He and Bruce became very close, and he had a big effect on the blossoming of Bruce's confidence in the last two months. Just being around him and watching how he works and prepares himself was a special experience, one I'll never forget.

Some things work out for the best in funny ways, just as my ejection in Chicago turned out to be positive. Even though I'd failed to get my twentieth win before my family and friends in Texas, in some ways when I did get it, it was even better—it came before the Boston fans, and ironically, it came exactly one year to the day (August 30) after my surgery in Columbus, Georgia [and one day from being two years from the day that he walked off the mound in Cleveland]. It wasn't all easy. Buck and I got mixed up on a coverage at first, which preceded a two-run homer by Carmen Castillo. I had some blister problems. But I struck out eleven Indians, including the side in my last inning (the seventh), and had the 7–3 win. It was also ironic that Kosc was umpiring at first base. But all that aside, I was most happy to not only get that out of the way so I could concentrate on nothing but winning the division, but we could also put an end to the rut that had seen us lose five out of six. Again my teammates made it worthwhile, making me feel as if they were as happy as I was to be a twenty-game winner. We still had only a 3½ lead because Toronto was in the midst of a nine-game winning streak and was becoming the last team to mount its challenge; but somehow I couldn't be worried.

And I was right. The next time we lost was September 11, and by then the lead had ballooned to nine games.

·7·
SEPTEMBER'S
GLORY

"When I was playing, I always said that a pitcher should never be the MVP over an everyday player. Then I became a manager, and quickly found out how important one great starting pitcher is to an entire team. Let's see the American League East standings with Roger Clemens pitching for either the Yankees, Blue Jays, Indians, or Tigers."

—Lou Piniella,
Yankees' Manager

ALL SEASON long, we'd been holding off challenges, and the last one was by Toronto. They were 3½ games back on September 1, and right about then we read some quotes by the Twins' manager Ray Miller essentially claiming that the Blue Jays were a far superior team, would catch us, and would win going away. After I got my twentieth on August 30, we then finished off Cleveland 4–3—when Calvin struck out four of the last five batters—and swept the Rangers three straight: 6–4, 8–6, and 4–3. On September 4, the Mets came in for an exhibition game that sold out Fenway, brought out more than one hundred media people, and caused as much excitement as if the Yankees were in town. I posed for pictures with Gooden, we all got asked questions about playing one another in October, and I swear there were more Mets fans than Red Sox fans in the stands.

We had won five in a row and had the lead back up to 5½ over Toronto when Miller and the Twins came into Fenway on September 5. Miller apparently was besieged with questions and denied that he said what was written. (Marty put him down by saying, "What do I care what Ray Miller said? He's about to be fired.") I couldn't have cared less about what he did or didn't say. We did care about Toronto, because the Red Sox and Blue Jays haven't gotten along too well and a few of their players had popped off and said they were better. All that did—once again—was motivate us further.

My next start was the opener of the Twins series. All I had to do was make sure I got our hitters back to the dugout as quickly as possible. Rice hit a grand slam, Barrett hit a three-run homer, and my win number 21 was a 12–2 breeze. Everything was working for us at that point, and by then people could see that if our lineup was healthy, there wasn't a better team in the league. We had guys who were hot who didn't even get the credit for being big hitters— guys such as Barrett, who was as good a clutch hitter as there was. The guys who were supposed to carry us at that point were all hitting together, too, and the team was incredible. The winning streak eventually reached eleven games, and at times I actually was awed by the way everyone was swinging the bat.

As a pitcher, I can look at a hitter and see that he's on every pitch, and we had a whole team of hitters right on every pitch for almost two weeks. It was like the roll the Giants were on heading to the Super Bowl. Rice hit 2 grand slams in three games at one point, belted 9 homers and knocked in 32 runs in twenty-four games and was as hot as he had been all season; when a man has 200 hits, knocks in 110 runs, and has 303 total bases, he's got to be somewhat hot all season. Buckner hit 5 homers in three games. We swept the Twins, scoring 24 runs in three games. Then we went into Baltimore and beat them 9–3 (in eleven innings) and 7–5—as Evans hit 3 homers in the two nights—before I was to try to up the streak to eleven in pursuit of win number 22.

There is a reason that our hitters performed so well: work. Those guys work and work and work. Guys such as Buckner, Evans, Boggs, Gedman, and Barrett spend extra hours every week with Hriniak, and others, such as Rice, work with Johnny Pesky. I love to sit out underneath the center field bleachers and watch and listen to what Walter puts them through, because it's fascinating. I've soaked up enough so I feel I can help high school kids' thinking on hitting.

Buckner is absolutely amazing. Everyone used to kid him by saying that he looks like a sailor with a wooden leg on a rolling ship deck. You could hear everyone saying "come on, come on" when he'd be rounding third trying to score on a base hit. He'd be digging his heart out, and then when he'd get to the plate, he'd try that headfirst slide, stick, and not go anywhere. He's accused of not having speed, but he leads the team in doubles every year. What he does to get himself ready to play is amazing. I'll come in four hours before a game, and he's already there. He soaks his feet and ankles in ice for more than an hour before the game, a half-hour after every game, and goes through a complicated set of stretching exercises, just so he can play. That just shows how much he loves the game. Near the end of the season, he was taking whirlpool ice baths, which was a first in my experience. He'd throw a bucket of ice in the whirlpool. He told me to try it once, which I did, but I couldn't stay in there more than ten seconds—and I ice down my arm every day. The thing was about 45 or 50 degrees. I guess it's great for his muscles, numbs up his body, and speeds up his healing. You'll see him running in the outfield in his shorts, pulling one shoe on, hurrying around the clubhouse. He's got his locker spread out over about four others. What a character. He's always talking during a game. Sometimes I'll make a throw to first base and he'll ask me to turn it down a notch. He'll come over and tell me what everyone on first base is talking about. Marty is a great talker too, and I'll get him in on some of the pitches. I'll ask Marty what he wants me to throw, and when I'm successful with his pitch, he'll come into the dugout and say that he feels as if he threw the pitch. I do that about once every two games in a big spot. I like doing things like that, because you've got to have fun.

Evans is very quiet and is another one of the guys who works so hard. The amazing thing about him is his fielding. He plays right field *so* well, which is no easy feat. I didn't see him in all his gold glove days, but he plays that very difficult area as if it's his. Because of the ground you have to cover, the sun, and the angles, if you stick someone inexperienced out there and ask him to play that cul-de-sac, you'll see the ball running all around the place.

So, all our big hitters were rolling together when we hit Baltimore, which made us feel nearly unbeatable. But the day I was to pitch and try to get the streak to eleven wins in a row, I had one of the great thrills in my life. After the 7–5 win (Tuesday, September 9), Baylor asked me if I wanted to go to Washington and meet the President at the White House the next morning. "Are you crazy?" I replied. "Of course. I wouldn't miss it for the world." On the bus back to the hotel, a couple of people asked me how I could go on the day I was going to pitch. Well, how many times does a person get the chance to meet the President of the United States? It was a

once-in-a-lifetime deal, part of the fun that goes with what I do—
and I'm not going to blow that. I may not have an opportunity like
this when I'm out of baseball, so I might as well enjoy everything
I can while I have the chance.

Baylor; Joe Sambito; Mike Greenwell; Nip; Jack Rogers and his
wife, Ellie; Red Sox radio announcer Ken Coleman and his wife,
Ellen; Coleman's partner Joe Castiglione; and I were all supposed
to meet at 10:30 and be picked up by two limousines at our hotel
in Baltimore. I got down there close to 10:25. No Nip. I dialed his
room. His phone was busy. So I ran up and began banging on his
door. He'd decided to sleep in rather than go. "Come on," I yelled
at him. "You've got five minutes. You'll never get this chance again."
He threw on his Johnny Dangerously outfit—a pin-striped suit with
a red tie and pointed shoes. His hair was still wet and he had to
finish dressing in the limo, but he made it. "Nip, the Secret Service
won't let you through the gate looking like Johnny Dangerously,"
I told him. "They'll frisk you for sure."

When we went through the doors to the White House, the marine
guard turned out to be a Red Sox fan. Here *we* are, big-eyed, going
into the Roosevelt Room, and the guard's eyes lit up like light bulbs.
You could see he was anxious to talk to us, but he couldn't move.
Unfortunately, we sort of ignored him because we were so excited.
He got the word around, though, because almost a minute after
we got to the Roosevelt Room there were other guards outside,
wanting autographs. I think they knew we were coming, because
the visit was arranged by Tim Samway, a man we know at the park
whose brother works in security at the White House.

The president of Brazil was there at the same time we were, and
Nancy Reagan was entertaining his wife. Reagan had to meet with
the Brazilian president at one or two. It was just before noon when
we sat down to eat at a table that must have seated twenty. All
of a sudden the door opened, and in came the President. It was
as exciting as I dreamed as a kid. I kept looking at Nip, saying,
"You owe me." Reagan went around and introduced himself to everyone. Baylor had a hat (size 7) for him. Sambito gave him a jacket.
We had him autograph some balls, and Sambito told him that he
needed to practice on writing on baseballs. We gave him some team-
autographed balls, and I had one of my twenty-K balls for him.
When he got around to me, I said, "Nice to meet you, sir, I'm Roger
Clemens and I'd like to present you with one of the balls from the

game when I set a major league record for strikeouts." Reagan looked at me, took what was in my hand, and said, "Well, thank you very much. . . ."

He didn't realize what I'd given him at first. We all talked for about twenty-five minutes, but he had to eat lunch with the president of Brazil. He talked about how he played with Hall of Fame pitcher Grover Cleveland Alexander in the movie *The Winning Season*, and how he had been a radio sports announcer and he'd do those recreations after the play-by-play came across the Western Union ticker. He told us about the time he had to make up the ninth inning because with two outs and two strikes in the ninth, tie game, man on third, the darned wire went out. He had the guy fouling one pitch after another, just missing home runs. He got to a full count and couldn't go anywhere with it.

"Every time I go to an Orioles game, they lose," Reagan told Baylor.

"It doesn't matter tonight," Baylor shot back, "Rocket's pitching." I cracked up.

Reagan had some adviser there who kept rushing him along. He was trying to stay and talk baseball, and this guy kept saying, "Sir, you've got to get going." Sambito told Reagan, "Libya will still be there. Daniloff will still be in jail. Push everything back a day and stick around with us."

Reagan went right across the hall into the Oval Office, so we got a little glimpse of that. The Secret Service guys later told me that as soon as he got back in there, he looked in his hand, remembered the twenty-K game, and realized what he had. He then personally sent me a picture and a handwritten letter. He didn't send anyone else one, and Tim Samway's brother told him that Reagan had made a mistake in protocol by not having a letter sent to everyone; but he just fired my note off. How many kids from Vandalia get personal notes from the President?

Reagan left and five minutes into lunch, in popped George Bush. I had met him twice before, back home at Spring Woods in 1980 when I was a senior and he was running for vice president, and again at the All-Star Game. At the latter, I was wearing my "United States of Texas" T-shirt, so he had a picture taken of the two of us together. "You don't know how glad I am that you're doing so well," he told us, because he is originally from Connecticut and now lives in Maine. He was embarrassed at the All-Star Game when he threw out the first ball because he had on a protective flak jacket and couldn't throw well. He was a great baseball player at Yale, the captain of the 1948 team with former Red Sox pitcher Frank Quinn; they had finished second in the country, to Southern Cal. He also said that too many people around him—from Yale to Washington—were New Yorkers.

Out he went and in came Donald Regan. "Aren't they ever going to let us eat?" Nip mumbled—laughing, of course. Regan was a Bostonian and also talked about how glad he was that we were in first place. He clearly had the air of a man of power, one of those people you automatically listen to. When Regan left, I told Nip, "We have met the President, the vice president, the Speaker of the House [Tip O'Neill, at the game the night before], and the man behind all the power. You *really* owe me." Not only that, but Bush, O'Neill, and Regan were all Red Sox fans. Baylor later said that this means that we won't get audited in 1987. Nip tried to claim that Reagan said he wanted the Sox to "win one for the Nipper," but no one believed him.

When we ate, Nip and I had a little fun. We made John Belushi eyes at each other, and I'd say, "Look at that Nobel Peace Prize," and pretend to stick a plate or a piece of silverware in my pocket, and Nip would do the same. Not that you can get out of there with anything; coming and going, you have to go through a guardhouse and be weighed. Anyway, the Secret Service guys gave us key chains and tie clips with the presidential insignia, and they sent us pictures and videos of the visit. When I showed the video to my mother, she was in awe.

When we finished lunch, we looked at the Nobel Prize in the Roosevelt Room, then took a tour, which as far as I was concerned was the ultimate field trip. I wish I'd had a tape recorder so I could have taped what the Secret Service men said. They told us about every room, explained everything. My mother and grandmother would love it, especially one room where they displayed the china from every President since George Washington.

We went into the pressroom, which the guards told us was where Amy Carter used to roller skate. In the Yellow Room, we were shown a painting they thought had been burned, was found, bought in France for $11, given back to the White House, and is now worth millions. Nip and I got on either end. "OK, Nip, you get on that end, I'll get this one," I said, and we pretended that we were going to make off with it. "It's worth giving up two runs," I told Nip

on the drive back up to Baltimore. As soon as I got back to the
hotel, I called home and told my mother and brothers and sisters
all about the visit; I'm still a country kid who came from nowhere
for whom this was an experience they couldn't believe, especially
my grandmother.

The White House experience compares to seeing the "last-wish"
kids at Children's Hospital or the Dana-Farber Cancer Center. Kathy
O'Kane at Children's Hospital in September had told me that there
was a kid from Texas who had only a few days to live and who
wanted to meet me, so I went over after batting practice in my uniform, before I ran. Most nights Nip and I go out at six, after BP,
and run down Boylston Street, into the park in the Fens and do
a couple of miles; the hospitals are right up the street. The kids
like to see me in the uniform. Early in the year I showed up about
2:30 in my jeans, and a couple of the kids asked, "Is that really
Roger Clemens?" When I come in the uniform, I guess I'm more
real to them, and it's then that I really get the "Christmas-eyes"
looks. Being able to make someone happy like that is truly exciting.
It hurts when I think they can't ever experience even a Little League
game. I'm in a situation right now where I can help. When I'm retired, I won't have the same impact; so I want to do it now. Boggs'
heart is always in the right place, too. He does a great deal for
multiple sclerosis in the Tampa area since he learned last January
his sister has it. So I took the money I got from the T-shirt sales
and sent it to them. I have also tried to get involved with the Sun-
shine Kids in Houston. I gave them the MVP van from the All-
Star Game, for instance. Baseball players have a rare opportunity
to do something for society. Life's been good to me, and I want it
to be good for others. If a ballplayer ignores a last-wish kid, he's
abusing his privilege. I can't forget where I came from. What fasci-
nates me is that most of the parents I meet are special. I don't know
if I could handle some of the things they go through, and I only
hope that some of them realize how much respect I have for them.

I'd have concentrated a lot more in the game that night after our
visit to the White House if we weren't up by ten games, but the
way the team was hitting, it didn't seem to matter. I struggled all
night. I had problems with the mound, didn't feel comfortable, and
allowed four runs in the second inning to put us down 4–3. I settled

down after that, pitched six innings, and Rice, Gedman, and Henderson all homered for a 9–4 win that Calvin saved. That was eleven in a row, and I was up to 22–4. What a day.

When we left Baltimore, we went to New York and Milwaukee before going to Toronto to try and put it away. The Yankees beat us two out of three, and on that Saturday, September 13, we ended up in the stands. It was the eighth and I had been doing my arm weights up in the clubhouse between innings. I was on my way back down when Spike and Jimmy collided by the stands down the left field line. Spike was being helped off by Charlie Moss, so I went to help walk Spike up to the clubhouse. When I met him at the bat rack, I heard a ruckus going on down the line, looked up, and players were looking into the stands. All of us jumped out of the dugout and took off down the line. What happened was that while Jimmy and Spike were lying there, two fans were fighting over Jimmy's hat, which they'd stolen by leaning over the rail. After Jimmy got up, he said, "Give me my hat back; I'll go get you another one and autograph it right here."

The guy shouted, "——— you, nigger, come and get it." Jimmy was three rows deep in a hurry. Jim Rice is one of the easiest-going people in the world. He had offered to give the guy a new cap and everything, and the guy shouts racial obscenities at him. He *had* to go into the stands when the guy said that. Fish and some others were standing there, and I blew by them and hurdled the railing. I found myself in the second row, and some guy came at me. I didn't know why he was coming at me, but I threw up my forearm and he fell over about four seats. I went up and people got real friendly in a hurry. It was crazy, but Mac, Jimmy, and I felt it was something we had to do because of what the fan had yelled. Marty said he had to stay on the field and guard the hats and gloves. Thank goodness no player or fan was hurt.

We then swept Milwaukee four straight back home in Fenway, and they got me my twenty-third. This again was one of those games where Mac did precisely what he had promised in June — left me out there to win or lose my own game. Juan Nieves pitched very well for the Brewers, but Evans beat him with a seventh-inning homer, and I held on, 2–1. That meant that we headed for Toronto with a 10½ game lead, so one win basically would end it.

One thing that was trying from late August on was the MVP controversy. Writers constantly were asking me about it, and what worried me was that anything I said would come out as a knock at Jim Rice, which is the last thing I wanted. In the first place, from the day I arrived in the clubhouse in Boston, he has been great to me and has been a sincere, close friend. In the second place, the man is one of the best players in baseball, a probable Hall of Famer. I didn't want it to be him versus me. MVP. There were pitchers one or two wins behind me, and I was reading how I was a shoo-in for the Cy Young, so I had to put it out of my mind and hope that no one thought *I* was thinking that way. Well, one person did. Sparky Anderson said, "I don't know how he thinks he has it locked in, because Jack Morris is going to win it." If I answer most questions, I can get into trouble, because somehow the answers are not the same in black and white. I almost like radio and television interviews better, because at least the inflection of my voice comes through. How many times do you hear players on a bus or in a clubhouse talking about how they think some guy's popping off when they read his quote in the paper? I learned about those mistakes as a rookie, when some veterans thought I was knocking the bull pen. So I learned and grew from that experience, the same way I learned and grew from the umpiring experience with Kosc. And I hope I learn and grow from pitching experiences such as the mistake I made to Petralli in Texas.

The business of whether or not a pitcher can or can't be the MVP is something I couldn't personally answer. But I did read a *Sports Illustrated* story about the history of the award, so inside I certainly felt that I had a chance, along with Rice. I appreciated the significance of the award. As Baylor, who won in 1979 when he was playing for California, always said, "Wherever I go, I'll always be *an* MVP."

That *SI* article ["It's Oscar Time for Baseball," September 8, 1986, issue] contained a number of observations I found interesting. For example, 1973 winner Reggie Jackson said, "The MVP isn't some publicity contest winner, like the Heisman Trophy winner. It isn't the *best* player, either. I guess it would be the player who did the most to help his team win." George Brett, the 1980 winner, claimed, "The Most Valuable Player should be in a pennant race; then you look at that team. If you took him out of the lineup or took him off the team, would they be in the pennant race?"

Sparky Anderson maintained that the MVP should come from a first-place team, period. I tended to agree with that. If I were 30–0 and we finished third, how valuable could I have been? That was my argument in stating that Rice deserved the MVP more than Mattingly, while Mattingly certainly was the player of the year. "I might not have seen it this way as a player," Yankees' manager Lou Piniella was quoted as saying, "but as a manager, believe me, if you have the great pitcher to throw out there every fifth day, it's invaluable."

There were other factors cited. "Impact" and "leadership" were mentioned. Rice said simply, "The player with the best stats should win." The article claimed that some years — as was the case when Willie Stargell tied the Cardinals' Keith Hernandez in 1979 as a reward for being the leader of Pittsburgh's "Fam-i-lee" — pure leadership is a factor. Nineteen seventy-three winner Pete Rose pointed out that, in 1970, leadership was ignored when Tony Perez was beaten out by teammate Johnny Bench. In evaluating a player, Gene Mauch would ask, "Where would a team finish with the guy?" I didn't realize that only once in the fifty-six years that the baseball writers have given this award has an American Leaguer won it on a second division team. [Rod Carew — with the fourth-place 1977 Twins. And not only did Carew hit .388 and knock in one hundred runs, but the Twins were within two games of first place right up to Labor Day. Three times (Hank Sauer once, and Ernie Banks twice), players from fifth-place teams have won it in the National. The only fourth-place American League finisher in the old eight-team league was pitcher Bobby Shantz of the '52 Athletics. The combined breakdown makes the significance of winning eminently clear: seventy-seven have come from first-place teams; twenty-one from second; seven, five, and three from third-, fourth-, and fifth-place clubs, respectively.]

As for the pitcher-as-MVP controversy, I found the guidelines — drawn up in 1938, according to Lang — that Baseball Writers Secretary-Treasurer Jack Lang mails out with the ballots interesting: 1) Actual value of player to his team, including offensive and defensive contributions. 2) Number of games played. 3) General character, disposition (Ballard Smith take note), loyalty, and effort.

The *SI* story stated that because a Cleveland writer had said he could not vote for a pitcher in the late fifties, an amendment has been added that says, "All players are eligible, including pitchers, both starters and relievers." To further emphasize that point, when Lang notifies each writer of his voting committee appointment in July, he stipulates that "if you feel that you can't vote for a pitcher for MVP, tell me and I'll put you on another committee." No writer can vote for both MVP and Cy Young. "We don't want trade-offs," said Lang. That apparently was in answer to all the players who say, "Pitchers have the Cy Young, our award is the MVP."

There were a lot of antipitcher sentiments, such as from the Angels' third baseman Doug DeCinces, another legitimate candidate. He differentiated between relievers and starters. "Relievers can be MVPs because they're in half the games. Starters go out every fourth or fifth day. No way." [After outfielders (thirty-four) and first basemen (nineteen), starting pitchers have won MVP awards more times (seventeen) than any other position. Before Ford Frick insisted on a separate-but-not-quite-equal award named after Cy Young in 1956—when, ironically, pitcher Don Newcombe still won the MVP—starters were common winners, including three successive seasons in the American League with Spud Chandler (1943) and Hal Newhouser (1944–45). Since the Cy Young was initiated, Sandy Koufax, Denny McLain, Bob Gibson, and Vida Blue have all won MVP awards.]

The one remark in the article that angered me was from Brett, who said, "I don't think it should be a pitcher. That's why they have a Cy Young Award so the guys who sit around in the bull pen and the dugout and do crossword puzzles and eat nachos and come up to the clubhouse and practice their putting stroke or get in attendance pools every night—so those guys can have their own award. The Most Valuable Player should be a guy who goes out and plays every day." If Brett thinks all we do is eat nachos, let him come along and follow my program with me for a week or two. I presume he was being funny—because he is a very funny person—but my first reaction was to take it the wrong way and get my back up in defense of all pitchers. After a while, I kept wishing we'd clinch so we could forget the whole MVP business and concentrate on the team, the play-offs, and the World Series.

As it turned out, my start in Toronto—the third game, Sunday, September 21—had some importance. We lost the first two games of the series. Seaver unfortunately sprained a ligament in his right knee on Friday night and had to leave, an injury that at the time no one realized would deprive him of the chance to pitch against the Mets in the Series and rob us of the opportunity to use him. The next day, Nip got drilled in the shin by a Moseby line drive. The way he got hit and went down, I was sure that he'd ruined his knee again. Fortunately, he was all right the next day, although you could count the stitches of the ball in his leg. After that game, the lead was still at 8½, but some people back home got a little nervous. "We don't have to worry because we'll turn it over to Roger," said Mac after the game. Some people think that puts pressure on me, but at that stage of the season, it relaxed me because it showed what confidence he has in me. I was pitching pretty well at the time, but Hurst was the best pitcher in the league. I wish I could tape every pitcher's "game face" on the day he's scheduled to start. I'd have taped Bruce the most, because for a period of a month and a half, he had it set in his mind exactly what he could do and couldn't do, and it showed as he walked into the clubhouse in his street clothes.

They tried a few things in Toronto. They didn't rub up a lot of the balls properly, so they were slippery. But Dave Sax homered early, Dwight made a great catch at the line off Mulliniks, and I got to the eighth, up 3–2. Fernandez singled to lead off the inning, but Mac was leaving me in to win or lose. They bunted him to second, but Moseby hit a sharp grounder to Boggs and I struck out Bell with a high fastball. Mac then turned it over to Calvin for the three outs, and we won 3–2. We knew we had the division won. Dwight said, "It's like Thanksgiving—you can smell the turkey cooking, you just can't wait to taste it." How true. [That was the fourteenth time that Clemens had won following a Boston loss.]

I hadn't had time to think much about the fact that I hadn't lost since the 1–0 game to the White Sox on August 4, that I was twenty games over .500, or that my only losses all season came in a thirty-three-day span. My focus was ahead, to clinching the division, enjoying that, and then getting ready for the play-offs and the likelihood of seeing Reggie, Witt, and the Angels once again.

We went to Milwaukee, lost the one game we played, then had a rainout. It was my turn against Toronto the next Friday night, September 26, knowing that all we had to do was win one game to clinch a tie and two to win it outright. On Friday night, Nip and I went to the Computer—Marty—in the outfield and ran the ticker tape through one ear and out the other and he told us what we had to do and that there was no way we wouldn't do it that weekend. He had his crystal ball in his locker and he started rubbing it; we went on the eleven-game streak, and he rubbed it every day thereafter. Lach had his Mr. Potato Head doll in his locker, and when we won, his head was facing forward or his hand was up; when we lost, his head was facing backward and his hand was down. Winning's a lot of fun.

What a game that Friday night one against Toronto turned out to be. Jimmy Key matched me pitch for pitch. Bell made a great throw to nail Evans at the plate in the seventh, and I left after nine in a scoreless tie before Barfield homered off Calvin in the twelfth for a 1–0 Toronto win. The way I looked at it, the important thing at that point was not to beat myself or my teammates; Key, Mark Eichhorn (who relieved Key), and the Jays simply beat us. Hurst went out the next afternoon and did what he did every start down the stretch, throwing a magnificent, gutsy 2–0 shutout that clinched the tie. When he threw his arms up after the last pitch, it gave me a thrill, because Bruce Hurst in my mind is — by age, experience, and character — the leader of the pitching staff.

We were all keyed up when we got to the park on Sunday, September 28, knowing that this was the day we could win it. Oil Can had it, too. He was really excited to have the chance to pitch the clincher, and it was a wonderful story that he came back from all he'd been through to do it and get his career-high sixteenth win. Boggs got to the two-hundred-hit plateau for the fourth straight year, and when he got his hundredth walk, they put on the message board that no one had had two hundred hits and one hundred walks since 1953 [Stan Musial]. We won it 12–3, and the celebration began.

As we were watching everyone celebrating, I sincerely felt happy for the older players — Rice, Baylor, Evans, Buckner, Armas — because they naturally feared that this might be their last shot. I went over and thanked Fish and Mac for what they did for me and the chance they gave me, and then Jimmy said that the fans were still in the park cheering and that we should go out and acknowledge them. So we ran back down the runway onto the field for what was an awesome ovation. One of the Boston policemen was on a horse named Timothy, and Rice yelled, "There's your horse, Tex, get on it." I looked up at the policeman, asked if I could get up there, and he said sure. When I got up and started riding around, the fans went crazy. I was looking for Deb, but couldn't find her.

I can imagine what the Red Sox and the fans would have thought if I had fallen off. I've been riding all my life, so they shouldn't have worried, but since I was in back of the policeman and far back on Timothy, I put too much pressure on his bladder, he started bucking, and I did nearly get thrown. I got off—in a hurry. Haywood Sullivan had a sense of humor about it. Leigh Montville of the *Globe* asked him if it was in my contract that I was prohibited from riding horses. "Only motorcycles," Sullivan responded. "Roger can ride a horse." I wonder if he knows that I have a motorcycle at home. . . .

Unfortunately, what a lot of people remember from that night was the show Nip and I did with Don Shane at Channel 4. I guess there were calls on all the talk shows about how drunk we were and how crazy we acted, but I wasn't even close to being intoxicated. In the celebration, I sprayed champagne, but all I drank was what ran down off my brow and went into my mouth. Deb and I went home for dinner, we joined the team at a local restaurant and had perhaps two cocktails, and took the limo to Channel 4. We watched Boggs do his Pee Wee Herman imitation on Channel 7, and we decided we'd have some fun too. We wore the sunglasses we'd bought three weeks earlier in New York and saved for the clinching, butted heads a couple of times, and acted a little crazy, but it was in good fun and wasn't some drunken scene. We were very excited. We might not go that way again.

That left us a week to get ready for California. But in my last start, on Wednesday, October 1, I got a terrible scare. I was pitching to Orioles catcher John Stefero in the second inning. Basically, all I was trying to do was get fine-tuned for the play-offs: work on my forkball and my with-seam fastball. I admit that I wasn't really complacent, but again I wasn't really sharp. I didn't have the fire to go right after people. I tried to run a ball at Stefero's thigh and let it run back, but I didn't get it in far enough and it ran right back over the middle. He threw the head of the bat out and drilled it right back at me. I saw it and tried to react by turning, as I wanted the ball to hit me in the back. My elbow was just there. It cracked really loud and ricocheted into right field, and my whole right arm got numb. I dropped my glove and stood there, with the end of my fingertips tingling. I could see the railroad tracks from the stitches on the ball.

As it turned out, I was lucky it hit me right on the elbow. If it had hit a little differently, it could have shattered the bone. Or, if it had hit the muscle, it could have bothered me for weeks. Nip accompanied me to the hospital for X rays, which turned out to be negative, and Dr. Pappas told me that a fraction of an inch one way or the other and I could have been done. The injury cost me the strikeout title and the pitching triple crown (wins, earned run average, strikeouts), but I was fortunate to get out alive. That left the last weekend to four games with the Yankees, which were anticlimactic since Boggs had a bad hamstring pull and couldn't go head-to-head with Mattingly to win the batting title. Some Yankees took cheap shots at Boggs, but Mattingly went up to Boggs and said, "Don't be stupid and try to play if you're hurt. The important thing is the play-offs. I wish I were in them."

I had to soak my elbow in ice every day and it was sore, but it seemed certain that I'd be able to start the play-off opener against the Angels. It had been a storybook season to that point — winning the division, going 24–4, winning the earned run average title, the twenty-K game, the All-Star Game — but I just wanted to get healthy and ready for what I anticipated would be the best part of it all. You play baseball to play in the World Series, and now I had a shot at it.

·8·
POSTSEASON DRAMA

"As I sat there in front of my locker after the sixth game, I couldn't help but think of the Angels. They went through the same thing. Now I feel for them, too, and I hope that the Mets respect us as much as I respect the Angels."

—*Roger Clemens*

AS THE final regular season weekend series with the Yankees wound down, I knew my elbow would be no problem in the play-offs. I went back and forth between the heated whirlpool and the ice and played some light catch. Although some fluid built up around the elbow, I knew after three days that I'd be physically ready to start the play-off opener with the Angels. What I didn't do right is blot everything out of my mind. I had all the running around because of the family, driving people to hotels, running sight-seeing tours and things like that, and I never got myself into the right frame of mind. Then, too, I let something else bother me. Sometime during that last week, three or four people whom I trust came up and asked if I'd heard what Gorman had said on the radio. They claimed that he was asked about the club's new policy of limiting pitchers to two-year contracts and why they'd only give Roger Clemens two years after the season he'd had and the promise he'd shown. They said that Gorman replied that he felt that I'm still a question mark because of my arm. He later denied it, but four of the people who told me are trustworthy, and I was infuriated. After all that we'd been through during the 1986 season, I was still a question mark? I couldn't get it out of my head. A couple of teammates told me not to worry about it, that Gorman just talks a lot, but I unfortunately let it affect me right on up until the opener against Witt, and my proper concentration was never there.

I tried to get myself pumped up, but it never felt right, and when I got to the mound, I heard everything. I saw everything from dugout to dugout. I noticed fans getting in and out of their seats in the crowd. I could see both dugouts, I watched Angels hitters coming up to the plate, I just wasn't zoned in the way I was when I struck out twenty; that night, I couldn't see anything but Geddy and the hitter. I got through the first inning of the play-off opener, but I had two runners on base and DeCinces made the final out by hitting a ball to the warning track in center. Then, in the second, I got the first two batters but I walked the eighth and ninth hitters, Bob Boone and Gary Pettis. That's not normal for me. Not only that, but it did me in. Ruppert Jones singled through the middle for the first run, Wally Joyner doubled to make it 2–0, and I was faced with Brian Downing for what was the out that had to keep us in the game, for any three- or four-run spot for either side would likely be the game. I had Downing one and two. He has an open stance and tries to pull the fastball on the inside half of the plate, often giving up the outer half if you can throw him a breaking ball out there. I threw him a slider that Geddy and I—and almost everyone on our club—thought was a strike. Larry Barnett called it a ball, and we did a lot of hollering. After the game, many reporters asked if that had been the key to the game, but it wasn't. One call doesn't make or break a game. I was the key, and I came back with a 2–2 fastball that Downing ripped off the base of the wall and we were down 4–0. That was enough for Witt, who not only had a shutout but a no-hitter into the sixth inning, finished with a five-hitter, and had the 8–1 win.

I settled down for a while during that game, but I was never the same after the second inning, and I left in the eighth when California scored three more runs. I was throwing hard, and while a lot of questions afterward focused on my physical condition, Reggie probably said it best when he described me as being "wild in the strike zone." I was fully aware of my problem that night and eventually cured it in my next start out in Anaheim, but we were down a game and Boone said that "beating Clemens is the key to the series." I didn't necessarily agree with that, because Hurst was the best pitcher in the league from August on, but we all realized how tough the Angels were. They'd beaten us seven out of twelve during the regular season, and their pitching had stopped us [the Angels held Boston to a .239 average in the twelve regular season games and had a staff earned run average against the Red Sox of 2.98, the best of any opponent]. So it was a difficult task.

To no one's surprise, Hurst won the second game on October 8 and took us to California, even at a victory apiece. Bruce called the 9–2 win "a nifty eleven-hitter," but with any luck he could have had about a five-hitter. He couldn't complain, though, because everything happened to California starter Kirk McCaskill. He lost a Boggs ground ball in the sun and a one-hopper down the third base line by Boggs that McCaskill later jokingly called a "ground-up." He didn't laugh at the time, because it scored a run. The Angels tied it when we made a couple of infield miscues and Joyner hit a homer into the bull pen. We would eventually get lucky and have Joyner miss the last four games of the series with an infected foot. He was swinging the bat the way he had the first two months of the season. We went ahead in the fifth when Grich lost a pop-up in the sun; then Grich got picked off rounding third in the sixth and got into it with the third base coach, Moose Stubing. Actually, Boggs made a great play cutting off Rice's throw, not only going deeper than he normally does for the cutoff, but making a leaping catch. The Angels then made a couple more errors in the seventh— one came when Evans' hustle sliding into second made Dick Schofield bounce his throw off Dwight's wrist and on into the dugout— and it became a rout.

At that point, all the media was asking whether or not I was going to start the fourth game on three days' rest. One group felt I should, because in a short series a manager should have his "best" out there three times and in the old days everyone started on the fourth day. Others felt I shouldn't be brought back, because I hadn't pitched on three days' rest all season and had thrown 144 pitches in the opener. Caught in the middle of all this was Nipper, who prepared himself to pitch the fourth game, but didn't know what was happening. I'd read and heard that I probably would pitch the fourth game, but Mac and Fish hadn't told me, and the situation with Nip got ticklish since he wanted to start it so badly. He was upset then, and eventually got very upset, which I understood. If I'd been in his shoes, I'd have wanted to have known what was going on, too. At one time I was told to do my work as if I were going on three days' rest, then another time I was told to proceed as if

I were going to go on my normal rest. There was a difference in preparation. On three days, I'd just play light catch between starts, whereas on four I'd do regular throwing. The only thing that I told Fish was that I felt good and that everything was on schedule. When we flew out to California after the second game, I geared my mind to work on three days' rest, just in case. And if they changed their minds, I'd do some distance running and throw for about five minutes on the off day.

It wasn't until the workout day (Thursday) that I was informed. I had told Nip that I'd let him know as soon as I was told, but the reporters all knew before I was officially given the word. I told Nip that if I'd had definite word, I'd have told him earlier, and he assured me that his being upset had nothing to do with me. He simply wanted the ball—badly—which is understandable.

The trip to Anaheim was fun, with Mrs. (Jean) Yawkey, Ted Williams, all the owners, and all the players' families. The problem was that there were so many people smoking that no matter where one sat, it felt as if it were right next to a fireplace; that's what made me sick on the flight home. Deb and I didn't do much out there. We played miniature golf a couple of times and went out to eat, but mainly we tried to get prepared for my next start. Can had the third game, and he pitched very well. When we got to the park, we all heard some story about his being in a car accident, but when he arrived—Can isn't known for showing up early—he said there was nothing to it. Apparently what happened was that Don Sutton was broadsided going to his office that morning, and when the report came out that "a pitcher" was in an accident, poor Can was naturally accused. It was simply an unfounded rumor, but one Boston television station (Channel 7) ran it before anyone got to the park and they could substantiate it, so Can's name was smeared again.

He was very excited, but no more so than I've seen him many other times. He had a 1–0 shutout into the sixth, when the Angels scored a run on Reggie's single. John Candelaria matched him at 1–1 into the seventh, and in the seventh Can made a couple of mistakes. He hung a breaking ball that Schofield hit out, walked Boone, and hung a screwball that Pettis hit out for a 4–1 lead. When he came out, Can was very upset with himself for getting beaten by the eighth, ninth, and first hitters; we lost 5–3, and I was coming back on three days' rest with us down 2–1 in games.

The three days' rest business meant almost nothing except a slight change in my between-start routine. What was important was to block everything out and not be the way I was in the opener, when I was cautious and thinking about a lot of things. That day, we decided that it was best that I not think about it all day, so we got up early and Nip and I went to the mall in the morning to have some fun. Nip felt a lot better then, but even if he didn't, he wouldn't have showed it because I was about to pitch and he's too much of a team man and a friend to be anything but supportive. He was pumping and encouraging me all day, and we were kidding each other, joking around and getting loosy-goosy. We both agreed that we were going to win, no matter what. Deb and Nip's girlfriend, Michelle, found us sitting outside, discussing the game, and Deb was worried that I wouldn't be ready. But I was. My intensity and jitterbugs were there right from the start. I was right back with Geddy from the start. It's always good to be a little jittery. I don't mean any kind of panic or a nervousness, but it helps to have a good feeling of excitement, because it helps the adrenaline. It always makes things look faster and quicker than they are, and when you're in the play-offs, everything is a little quicker and images are a lot sharper. It's funny. People kept asking me about the three days' rest, but I almost felt too strong and had to take some extra warm-up pitches in the bull pen before coming in.

Both sides were very quiet, with none of that "let's get him" noise in the dugout that we had in the first three games. Actually, there is a lot of respect between the Red Sox and Angels, mostly because there are so many veteran players on each team whom everyone admires. There was more tension in the play-offs than the World Series and very little was said in the clubhouse before games except for guys like Dwight, Baylor, and Rice telling the younger players what to expect in play-off baseball.

That night of the fourth game was unusually quiet, and there was a lot of concentration on every at bat, with our hitters trying to figure out what Don Sutton was doing. There's no question that getting off to a good start and striking out the first two Angel hitters settled me down and helped. I basically went out to the mound with the idea that I wanted to keep us in the game, concentrating on the first and fourth innings, leadoff hitters, two-out situations, and things like that. Sutton was his usual self, shutting us out into the sixth inning. But there we got one run when Buckner hit a clutch two-out double, and in the eighth we got two more when Barrett—who was setting all kinds of hitting records—singled in Spike and scored on a passed ball and an error. That gave me three runs to work with. Jones led off the eighth with a double, but I was able to strand him there. I believe that a pitcher usually gets three major tests in a game, and if he gets out of two of them, he'll succeed. The eighth inning was just my second test, so I figured I'd have one more in the ninth. I was right.

I'd thrown 143 pitches in the opener and was creeping past 125 into the ninth, but while my fastball had straightened out a little, I was still throwing hard. With the three-run lead, I just wanted to make people hit the ball. I threw DeCinces a little cross-seamer right across the plate, and while he hit it hard, at first I didn't think it was going out. But it carried out to center, which made it 3–1, so I concentrated on getting the other outs. George Hendrick grounded to Boggs, so I was two outs away. I had enough to finish; I just made the mistake of trying to get it over too quickly—a mistake I hope I never make again and a mistake Calvin repeated in the sixth game of the Series. I had Schofield and Boone 0 and 2 and made bad, careless pitches. I had them both, and attempted something a little different. I threw pitches that were too hittable in situations where they had to be swinging, and those were terrible mistakes, because with 0–2 counts and the game on the line, you never want to give up hits, especially to the eighth and ninth hitters in the order. Boone just got it over the infield, but it still was an 0–2 hit. McNamara came out and called for Calvin, and I walked off, disgusted. I watched in the dugout for two or three pitches, but then I decided that I had to get up into the clubhouse and ice my arm in case there was a seventh game. I listened to the radio in the trainer's room, right on through the inning as it got to 3–2. Then Calvin struck out Grich for the second out. Finally, I sat there in disbelief when the announcer said Calvin had hit Downing with the two-strike pitch. I couldn't figure out what was going on, what kind of pitch he had thrown. I just couldn't believe it. Cal later said that he got a brain cramp and decided to throw a curveball when Downing wasn't catching up to his gas, then he tried to throw the best curveball of his life. When I looked at it on the replay, it appeared as if it broke in on the batter like a screwball.

We eventually lost in the eleventh, and Calvin was very depressed. He must have stood in front of his locker answering questions for an hour, but I give him credit—he stood up to it. When it got tied up there in the ninth, I decided that the only thing for me to do was not dwell on the fourth game, but begin preparing myself for the seventh. I did some arm weights and sit-ups, and when the media surrounded my locker, I told them that I was getting ready for my next start and that I didn't want to dwell on our blowing the lead or being down 3–1. "I'll be up running in the morning and be ready for Wednesday," I told Fish. I knew that if something crazy happened and we did have a seventh game and I wasn't prepared, it would be worse than the feeling I had right then.

The fifth game was at noon Sunday, October 12, so I got up early and was out on the sidewalk running at seven. When I got to the park, I did some light throwing to get the lumps out and just kept thinking about one more start and one more chance to get us to the World Series. The atmosphere wasn't too happy, though; Hurst was also coming back on three days' rest. But after Gedman homered for a 2–0 lead, Bruce was tremendous. He got a tough break in the sixth when Grich hit a long fly ball that Hendu made a great effort to catch. He wouldn't have even been in the game if Armas hadn't hurt his ankle, but Hendu ran a long way, leaped, and as he hit the fence, had the ball deflect off his glove and over the fence.

The strange part of that was that Grich's ball looked like it was just a routine fly ball. Afterward, Bruce told me he couldn't believe that one had gone out or that a ball DeCinces hit carried to the fence in right center. For the entire series, even our hitters were talking about how the ball was jumping off the Angels' bats and carrying even when they didn't hit it well. Some of our players were convinced that they were corking their bats, and the talk got heavy that Sunday after Grich's homer. When we got back to Boston, DeCinces showed the TV camera the cupped end of his bat—with a wine cork stuck in it.

By the eighth inning of that fifth game, the Angels were up 5–2 and things looked pretty bad. We looked over there and Reggie had his arm around Gene Mauch, ready to come out. I went up to the clubhouse in the eighth and did some sit-ups. Can had been charting and came up, so we—plus Armas and someone else—went into the boiler room to watch the last two innings on television. Hurst was icing his arm in the trainer's room.

Witt was two outs away from clinching the pennant when Baylor hit his two-run shot. That was such a great moment, for Donnie doesn't hit Witt well. But for the last three innings, he went up and down the bench saying, "If this is going to be your last at bat of the season, make sure that you never wake up in the middle of the winter thinking that it wasn't as good as the best one you had all season." That's the way he approached it; when everyone else figured it was over, he refused to give up. Witt got Evans out, then Mauch took Witt out. We didn't second-guess the decision at the time. He'd thrown a lot of pitches, and we knew Geddy had already had a single, double, and homer off him that day. We were more interested in who was coming in—Gary Lucas—and who was coming up. As Lucas warmed up, I went to see Hurst, who was on the trainer's table. We talked a little bit about lifting weights to build up our legs over the winter, about how DeCinces' and Grich's balls had carried, and as I left to go watch the rest of the game, I told him that I didn't think it was time for the season to end. "It just doesn't feel as if it's time, not yet anyway," I said, and went back to the television.

I told everyone to stay in the same seats we had when Baylor had hit his homer. Lucas hit Geddy with the first pitch, and out came Mauch to bring in Moore to face Henderson. Hurst came in, and I was screaming at people to stay in the proper seat. As Moore warmed up—and later between innings—someone would go out into the clubhouse for a coke or a dip or a chew, and I told everyone we *had* to stay in the same seats. My seat was the couch, and with Henderson up, I kept sinking lower and lower. Everyone got very quiet when the count got to two strikes. I'll never know why Moore threw the forkball after throwing two fastballs by him. It was a nasty forkball, but it gave Hendu a chance, and he went down and got it perfectly. We all started yelling when he hit it, and when it went out, I turned to Can and hollered, "You're pitching, man, you're pitching. Give me a chance to come back Wednesday."

From Baylor's homer until the game was over, we had our hats in rally cap alignment—inside out and backward. Actually, we had them inside out and frontward for the top of the eleventh, inside out and backward for the bottom half. We scored the winning run and Calvin came back to shut them down for the save and the 7–6 win. Of course, it wasn't easy getting to Calvin. After Henderson put us ahead, Shag (Crawford) had it tied, with the bases loaded, one out, and a 2-and-0 count on DeCinces. Shag showed everyone something, for he jammed DeCinces to pop him up, got Grich, and got us into extra innings. When Al Michaels said, "If you're just tuning in now . . . too bad," in the tenth, he said it all. No one moved until the final out was made; then we ran down and joined in the celebration. It was as if we had won it all. Across the way, the Angels couldn't believe it. The clubhouse kids told us that when Moore got two strikes on Hendu, the home clubhouse kids popped a few bottles of champagne. I wonder if those kids still work there.

It was very quiet on the plane ride home, because everyone was both tired and drained. Unfortunately, that's where I got so sick. The smoke was unbearable. Nip, Sammy Stewart, and a few others kept moving around trying to find a spot away from the smoke, but they couldn't. We'd actually asked Jack Rogers if the smokers could have the front of the plane so there could be a nonsmoking area, but I guess it was impossible. My eyes started swelling and my shirt was soaked right through, and Deb had to get a towel and soak it in cold water. The allergy I have to cigarette smoke is such that when I break down, it's just like getting the flu. I've always had this allergy to smoke. When my family comes to my house, if they want to smoke, they go outside. We have a lot of smokers in our family, but they're very considerate. My mother would come into my room as a kid, and if she was smoking, I'd wake up from a dead sleep. Anyway, it knocked me out.

At that point, though, we had a pretty good feeling about winning the pennant. The Computer (Barrett) had said all along that if we could get the series back to Fenway, even down 3–2, we'd win it. In the sixth game, October 14, Can struggled through the first inning. He had the bases loaded and two out with two runs in and was basically in the same spot I had been in in the second inning of the first game. Then he made the big pitch, popping up Rob Wilfong, and breezed from there. McCaskill walked Boggs and Barrett to start the bottom of the first—handing us back the momentum—and once we tied it, we were on our way. In the third, we scored five runs as Spike, Boggs, Marty, and Buckner all got hits, Grich threw a ball away, and the 10–4 rout was on. We were even at 3–3, and I had another chance.

Randy was there with us, and I wanted to take my mind off the seventh game the way I had in Anaheim before the fourth game. I was pacing around the apartment from nine to eleven, raring to go. I didn't want to sit around too long and get tense, especially since I'd read that the Red Sox had never won a seventh game in Fenway Park. What I ended up doing for the first time in my life was flat-out predicting that we were going to win. I said, "I'm pitching tonight, I'm going to win." I also didn't want to think about the way my immune system had broken down and how sick I felt.

I knew that I had to keep momentum on our side from the beginning and that pitching against a tough, experienced, and proven winner such as Candelaria meant that a couple of early runs could be the game. The Angels, however, didn't play too well when they got back to Fenway. An error leading off the second gave us the first run, and when Boggs hit a two-out single through the box, it was 3–0. Hendu led off the fourth with a shot off Pettis's glove, and when Rice capped the inning with a three-run homer, I had a seven-run lead to coast with. I had been sick before the game, but there was no way I wasn't going to pitch. Mac asked me for only seven innings, and with my proper concentration, I had everything so scoped in that the illness never crossed my mind when I began throwing. I struck out only three, but I didn't have to worry about strikeouts with the lead. When we scored the three runs, I had to make certain that California didn't get the momentum back, and there I was able to strike out Grich to begin the third and establish that they weren't coming back.

By the the seventh, my legs were dead and my knees were quivering, as my strength just wasn't normal. I was pushing off with everything I had to keep my fastball going. Nip said that I didn't have any color and that I looked like a mummy. Mac wanted to take me out after the seventh, but I told him I still had pretty good stuff. I told him that if I didn't get the leadoff hitter out, he could come get me out of there. I gave up a single to Jones leading off, so as Mac was walking from the dugout to the mound, I turned and pointed to Cal in the bull pen, just like in the Texas days when I'd relieve in a Saturday game after going nine the night before. When Cal got in to the mound, I told him, "Go have fun. They seem to have slow bats tonight, so go get 'em." I went straight up to the clubhouse.

Usually I stick my arm in an ice bucket, but I had Rich wrap my elbow and shoulder in towels with ice and went to the back to Dr. Pappas's office. He came in and took my temperature, and I was shivering. He gave me some medicine, covered me up, and

THE SEVENTH ALCS GAME: OCTOBER 15, 1986

Red Sox, 8–1

CALIFORNIA	ab	r	h	bi	BOSTON	ab	r	h	bi
Jones rf	4	1	1	0	Boggs 3b	5	0	1	2
Wilfong 2b	1	0	0	0	Barrett 2b	4	0	0	0
Burleson 2b	3	0	2	0	Buckner 1b	2	0	1	0
Downing lf	3	0	1	0	Stapletn 1b	1	1	0	0
Jackson dh	4	0	0	0	Rice lf	4	2	1	3
DeCinces 3b	4	0	1	1	Baylor dh	4	1	2	0
Schfield ss	4	0	0	0	Evans rf	3	2	1	1
Pettis cf	4	0	0	0	Gedman c	4	0	0	1
Grich 1b	2	0	0	0	Hendersn cf	3	1	0	0
Howell ph	1	0	0	0	Owen ss	4	1	2	1
Boone c	2	0	1	0					
Narron ph	1	0	0	0					
Totals	**33**	**1**	**6**	**1**	**Totals**	**34**	**8**	**8**	**8**

California	000	000	010–1
Boston	030	400	10x–8

Game Winning RBI—Gedman (1).

E—Schofield, Pettis, Owen. DP—Boston 1. LOB—California 8, Boston 5. 2B—Baylor. HR—Rice (2), Evans (1). SB—Owen (1).

	IP	H	R	ER	BB	SO
California						
Candelaria (L 1-1)	3⅔	6	7	0	3	2
Sutton	3⅓	2	1	1	0	2
Moore	1	0	0	0	0	0
Boston						
Clemens (W 1-1)	7	4	1	1	1	3
Schiraldi	2	2	0	0	0	5

Clemens faced 1 batter in the 8th.

HBP—Boone by Clemens, Grich by Clemens.

Umpires—Home, Barnett; First, McCoy; Second, Garcia; Third, Bremigan; Left, Cooney; Right, Roe.

T—2:39. A—33,001.

I just lay there, shaking. The doctor said that my arm could bounce back all right, but when I got the flu, it didn't let the rest of my body bounce back. When Calvin closed the 8–1 game by striking out five of the last six batters, I was just lying there on the couch, covered with a blanket. I could hear everyone celebrating, so I stood up and tried to hug teammates and cheer along with them, but I got dizzy. I tried to stand up for the television interviews, but I had to sit down, and I must have sat there for nearly an hour talking to reporters.

It was still a great feeling, coming back from the dead. Marty had eleven hits and was sensational. Geddy had ten hits, knocked in six runs, threw out four runners in big situations, and was the backbone of the team. Spike and Baylor each had nine hits, and Calvin showed everyone what he was made of by bouncing back from the fourth game to finish the fifth and seventh games. I never thought too much about the Angels that night, but I would after the sixth game of the World Series. It's then that I realized how they felt, and with all the respect I have for Jackson, Grich, Boone, DeCinces, Sutton, Witt, and all of them, I know it was tough to get that far only to be denied the right to play in the World Series.

There was no celebrating for me. I just wanted to get home and get to bed, for the next morning we had to fly to New York to tape the Zest commercial. At that point, my body was rebounding, which it did for the next two or three days. The doctor kept telling me to hold back on my running, which I hated to do, but there was no choice if I wanted to maintain anything close to my normal strength. When we got out there on the field at Shea Stadium for the workout the day before the opener, we couldn't believe all the media. There was a lot in Boston in September and a lot for the play-offs, but this was incredible. There's nothing like the play-offs, but it's different from the glamour of the World Series, and every time I played golf this winter with Alan Ashby and Phil Garner of the Astros, they reminded me how lucky I am to have gone to the Series at the age of twenty-four when so many good players never get the chance.

Hursty was starting, so he was the center of attention. "I don't know how you did it all season," he kept saying to me. We also didn't know if Buck, with his high-top shoes that looked like they were from 1950 football days or made for a boxer, could play. He had hurt his Achilles tendon pretty badly in the seventh game against the Angels, so without the DH there was a chance that Baylor would play first, although Buck is one of the wonders of the world. When it came time for the World Series to begin, I figured he'd be in the lineup. And he was.

Charting that first game, October 18, was a treat, because both Hurst and Ron Darling were so good. Darling was throwing the ball great. He allowed only three hits in seven innings, but Hurst was on a roll. Bruce was throwing everything right where he wanted, but his forkball was dominating. I talked to Mookie this winter, and he said that when Hurst threw that forkball, it just never got to the plate. I didn't pick much up charting the game because there aren't many similarities between Hurst and me. I'd actually picked up more watching Mike Scott and Ryan pitch to them in the play-offs. Ryan was running a cut fastball away from them, Scott was using the forkball, of course, and Hurst was doing the same thing as Scott. I decided I'd use my forkball, too, but not because of Hurst's success. I struck out both Dykstra and Backman with forkballs, incidentally.

Darling showed his class afterward when he said, "Hurst did a better job than I did." When someone pointed out that the Boston run was unearned, he added, "Hurst still had to pitch a shutout, which I didn't." We got the run in the seventh without a hit. Darling walked Rice, then bounced a curveball off the corner of the plate to put Jimmy in scoring position. With two out, Geddy hit a ground ball that went right through Tim Teufel's legs for the run.

Mac brought Calvin in to pitch the ninth, and he started off the inning by walking Strawberry on five pitches. Spike went right over to him, just like they were back in Austin. "You've been here before, Nibbler," Spike said to him. "Just go get 'em." Spike and Calvin were very close in college, and Spike's always had the ability to say the right thing at the right time, and that was both the right thing and the right time for him to speak up. Knight tried to bunt Strawberry into scoring position, but Dave Stapleton got the bunt and made the force out at second; Stape may have been a forgotten man, but he played in every one of our postseason victories. Calvin then got Backman to fly out and struck out Rafael Santana. We had the opening win in Shea.

What I had been able to do in the fourth and seventh games of the play-offs, I didn't do in the second game of the World Series. The hype about my facing Gooden didn't bother me, because we'd been through it before at the All-Star Game. I honestly didn't think about its being *me* against *him* except when he was at the plate, because the Mets were enough to worry about. But when I got to the mound, I never established any rhythm of any kind. I had all kinds of prob-

lems with the mound, so I had no leg drive. I was trying to turn
my body and let the hitter see my numbers to try to maintain my
balance as I threw it, and I was all over the place. Not only that,
but I let it get to me. Maybe it was because I still didn't feel great
or something, but I never zoned in the way I should have, and I
learned a painful lesson. At least I chipped in to the offense. After
Spike walked to open the third, I got down a bunt that Hernandez
threw away at second. Boggs doubled in Spike, I scored my first
big league run when Marty singled, and Buck made it 3–0 with
a single.

However, I didn't do what I'm supposed to do after we score —
shut them down. I gave up a hit to Santana, then walked Gooden.
Now, Dwight is a dangerous hitter for a pitcher, but walk him?
Backman singled in a run, and Hernandez got the other run in when
he hit a liner off my leg. Boggs made a great play on the ball, bare-
handing it after it ricocheted off me. He made another good play
off Carter to end the inning and another in the sixth, and finally
people all across the country were seeing that he is a gold glove
third baseman. After all the work he's put into his defense, he
deserves every bit of credit he ever gets.

Henderson homered off Gooden in the fourth to make it 4–2,
and then Evans hit an unbelievable shot over the auxiliary press
box in left center for a 6–2 lead in the fifth. I still hadn't found
my rhythm, but I thought that with the lead I could get us through
the seventh. Evans made a good catch off Dykstra leading off the
bottom of the fifth. Then, when I walked Backman and Hernandez
singled, I looked up and Mac was heading for the mound. I wasn't
tired, and I didn't want to come out. But Mac told me that he felt
as if I were running out of gas and he wanted me to come back
early (with three days' rest) again and he didn't want me to throw
a lot of pitches. So out I went, without a chance to win it. I did
want to continue, but more important, I wanted to win, and both
Crawford and Stanley did terrific jobs in relief. We had a 9–3 win,
and there were some people in Vegas panicking.

When we got back to Boston, the fans were going wild. Unfortunately, the Mets came right back in Fenway and made it a three-
game series. I didn't know what was going on with Can's parents
at the time of the third game. I guess he'd gotten very upset when
his stepmother showed up with his mother and father, but while
he was extremely hyper in the first inning, I'd seen him like that

before and I didn't pick up on it. Can gave up four runs in the first and never recovered, although he pitched very well after the first problems. Every time he came in after an inning, Nip, Hursty, and I tried to pump him. Ojeda pitched a tremendous game. He was throwing change-ups like crazy and kept us off balance. He's developed a great pitch in that change. He threw it when he was with us, but not the way he does now. Our hitters were grumbling all night, and Bobby would come in with his fastball just enough to get everyone. The Mets won 7–1 and afterward had a few things to say about Can. At the press conference Monday, Can had said, "The Mets can be mastered . . . and I don't think Bobby Ojeda can be too confident pitching in Fenway."

With the lead in the Series, McNamara wisely decided to give Hurst and me our regular rest, which meant Nip got to start the fourth game, October 22. Nip was extremely excited just to be given the opportunity to start a World Series game, which—no matter how cool you try to remain—is a big thrill. He pitched well, too. He had them shut out into the fourth, when Carter hit a two-run homer, and he basically did his job—six innings, three runs. Darling just pitched better. Ron never gave in to our hitters. He got Evans with the bases loaded in the first, stranded Geddy after he doubled to lead off the second, and shut us out for seven innings before the bull pen finished the 6–2 Mets win. They evened the Series, but I felt happy that Nip got his opportunity and did his job. Anyway, I felt confident that we could win two out of three with Hurst, me, and Boyd each going with the full amount of rest.

And Hurst did it again. In the fifth game, he threw his forkball at every speed, and the Mets were freezing on his curveball, and he shut them out into the eighth, when he had a four-run lead. Gooden once again didn't really have it. Some hitters thought that he was dropping his arm, and Marty observed that where he normally is extremely fluid, that night he seemed uncomfortable and out of place. We got nine hits off him before he left without getting an out in the fifth, when it was 4–0. The funniest thing was Buckner hobbling around third and collapsing on home plate. Lachemann wanted to push him all the way down the line. Bruce had 15⅓ straight scoreless innings when Teufel hit a little fly ball down the right field line in the eighth that the wind blew into the stands. They got another run in the ninth and had two on, but Bruce bore down and blew the ball by Dykstra with all the confidence in the world. "The best thing about tonight is that Hurst is done for the Series," praised Hernandez. That turned out to be an ironic statement, especially coming from him.

I felt certain that we would win that sixth game. I was completely recovered from the flu, and my body was back to normal. Seaver had talked to me about the mound, noticed that I needed to swing my leg two inches higher, and that was worked out. It should have been perfect. People ask me if I regret anything aside from not winning. Sure, I'd have liked to have continued through the eighth. I wish I'd bunted better in the sixth game. But I think the only thing I really look back on with regret is that I didn't pitch in the seventh game. I'm not second-guessing the manager when I say I wish I'd gotten the call at 3–3 in the seventh inning and let Calvin close out the ninth; that's just the way my heart feels.

Ojeda deserves a lot of credit for holding on in the sixth game and not letting us put it away. He got some help. Evans' ball off the fence in left center in the first inning *could* have been a home run and it would have been 3–0 instead of 1–0 before they ever got up, and the last out of the inning was a line drive Geddy hit to Strawberry. If I'd have gotten the bunt down in the second in between the hits by Spike, Boggs, and Barrett, maybe we'd have had two runs instead of one. On that at bat, I couldn't believe that Ojeda threw me a change-up. Before I went up there, I asked the Computer (Marty), "Do you think he'd ever throw me—the opposing pitcher—a change-up?" Marty said, "Ojeda will throw *anyone* a change-up." I got up there, got the green light to swing, and fouled off a ball. The problem was that I couldn't figure out if that pitch had been a change-up or a mediocre fastball. I soon found out. I squared to bunt and it seemed as if the pitch never arrived. It had a parachute on the end of it, and I lunged and popped it up to Carter. "See, I told you," said Marty as I walked back to the dugout.

Then came all the rest—the blister, the lead, the 1-2-3 seventh, then Greenwell pinch-hitting for me in the eighth. I can still see the "Congratulations, Boston Red Sox" that flashed on the message board with two out in the tenth, and all the bizarre plays. I'm glad I stopped our clubhouse kids from opening the champagne in the tenth, and I'll never forget Marty's saying, "Somewhere, Gene Mauch is smiling."

The ending still seems like a blur. We all went from the high of Henderson's homer and the 5–3 lead on Marty's single, to two

THE SIXTH GAME OF THE WORLD SERIES: OCTOBER 25, 1986

Mets, 6–5

BOSTON	ab	r	h	bi
Boggs 3b	5	2	3	0
Barrett 2b	4	1	3	2
Buckner 1b	5	0	0	0
Rice lf	5	0	0	0
Evans rf	4	0	1	2
Gedman c	5	0	1	0
Hendersn cf	5	1	2	1
Owen ss	4	1	3	0
Clemens p	3	0	0	0
Greenwll ph	1	0	0	0
Schiraldi p	1	0	0	0
Stanley p	0	0	0	0

NEW YORK	ab	r	h	bi
Dykstra cf	4	0	0	0
Backman 2b	4	0	1	0
Hernandz 1b	4	0	1	0
Carter c	4	1	1	1
Strwbrry rf	2	1	0	0
Aquilera p	0	0	0	0
Mitchell ph	1	1	1	0
Knight 3b	4	2	2	2
Wilson lf	5	0	1	0
Santana ss	1	0	0	0
Heep ph	1	0	0	0
Elster ss	1	0	0	0
Jhnsn ph-ss	1	0	0	0
Ojeda p	2	0	0	0
McDowell p	0	0	0	0
Orosco p	0	0	0	0
Mzzlli ph-rf	2	1	1	0

Totals	**42**	**5**	**13**	**5**
Totals	**36**	**6**	**8**	**3**

```
Boston       110  000  100   2-5
New York     000  020  010   3-6
```

Game Winning RBI—None.

DP—Boston 1, New York 1. LOB—Boston 14, New York 8. 2B—Evans, Boggs. HR—Henderson (2). SB—Strawberry 2 (3). CS—None. S—Owen, Dykstra, Backman. SF—Carter.

	IP	H	R	ER	BB	SO
Boston						
Clemens	7	4	2	1	2	8
Schiraldi (L 0-1)	2⅔	4	4	3	2	1
Stanley	0	0	0	0	0	0
New York						
Ojeda	6	8	2	2	2	3
McDowell	1⅔	2	1	0	3	1
Orosco	⅓	0	0	0	0	0
Aguilera (W 1-0)	2	3	2	2	0	3

Stanley faced 1 batter in the 10th.

HBP—Buckner by Aguilera. WP—Stanley.

Umpires—Home, Ford (AL); First, Kibler (NL); Second, Evans (AL); Third, Wendelstedt (NL); Left, Brinkman (AL); Right, Montague (NL).

T—4:02. A—55,078.

out and none on in the bottom of the inning—one out and one strike from the World Championship with everyone braced to charge the field . . . Calvin was *so* close, with the two strikes on Carter when he singled. And Mitchell singled. Calvin learned— the way I learned in the fourth game of the play-offs—that you can't try to get the game over too quickly. That's what happened with Carter. And after Mitchell's single, he had two strikes on Knight, only to have the same thing happen. Single. 5–4. Calvin was pretty tired at that point. He's basically a three- to six-out pitcher, so Mac went to Stanley, who'd pitched well throughout the play-offs. He, too, got two strikes on Mookie, and I couldn't see what happened— where Geddy set up, where the pitch was— except that all of a sudden the ball was bounding back to the screen and Mitchell was scoring. Then the ball took the funny hop through Buckner's legs. . . . Talk about an autumn chill. . . .

I was angry at the security guards who were yelling at Calvin when he came off the field, and I'd really get angry when I found out later that people were lobbing firecrackers, and security guards were cursing out the wives and families. I was also numb, sitting there in front of my locker for nearly a half-hour. Actually, I had thought about the seventh game when it was still 3–2, because I iced my arm down longer than usual, trying to numb it so it could bounce back in less than twenty-four hours. The extra day of rain definitely helped, and Sunday night I iced my arm for about a half-hour in the room. I got a bucket of ice from the machine, wrapped it in towels, applied it myself, sat on the floor, and watched television. I wanted another chance, badly.

The next afternoon I took Deb to the airport. It was raining, so I figured we weren't going to play, and I had the cab go on another mile to Shea and did my running. A lot of hitters had come out to work. The off day did us good and gave us a chance to regroup. Nip and I were going to get something to eat early that night, but as I was coming down the elevator to meet him, someone told me that Mac had announced that Hurst was starting the seventh game instead of Can. When I got downstairs, Nip had already taken off to talk to Can and try to console him. No matter what had happened one night in July, Nip felt a strong kinship with Can, and he was determined to do his best to help him out.

Bruce did his job, too. We had our chances to blow it open early again, but Sid Fernandez came in and blew us away to keep them within three runs. Hursty would have gotten us to the seventh with a 3–1 lead, too, but he tried to do one thing with Hernandez and he poked it into left center. It was a cross-seamer up in his eyes, which was the only pitch he wished he could have had back.

It was exciting sitting in the bull pen the whole game. Every time the phone rang, I jumped. But they decided to go with Calvin to start the seventh at 3–3. Nibbler threw the ball extremely well, but I think he and Joe wanted to beat the Mets more than anything, and it might have worked against them. He might have overthrown the ball, and Knight greeted him with the homer. They got two more for the 6–3 lead. Calvin may have tried too hard, but Strawberry had no call to say "that's why we got rid of Schiraldi" after the game. Evans, who had a great Series, got us back to 6–5 in the eighth, but Jesse Orosco came in and got three straight hitters, Mac went to Nip in the eighth, Strawberry homered, and they had it, 8–5.

I never got to pitch again, unfortunately, and then came all the garbage after the game with Jack's getting hit and the police laughing at us. . . . It wasn't all bad. Hurst went in to congratulate Ojeda, and they had an embrace—a moment that Channel 5 caught and none of us will ever forget. Bruce, Bobby, and John Tudor went through a lot together that the rest of us can't ever appreciate, and there is a bond among them the way there is a bond among Bruce, Nip, Can, and me.

About a month later, I got a letter from a Red Sox fan that had the calculations on the odds of our losing that sixth game with two outs and two strikes on two different guys with a two-run lead. The guy wrote that the odds were two hundred something thousand to one.

"Do you realize how impossible it was to lose that game?" he wrote.

I'd rather not think about it any more. I've got my next start in 1987 to think about.

EPILOGUE

*"When we didn't win with that team we put in the
field in 1977, 1978, and 1979, I sat everyone down and
said, 'We must be doing something wrong.' The answer
was that we had it backward. We had the star players.
We didn't have the pitching. That's when we decided
that there was one Red Sox tradition that had to
change: that this was first and foremost a hitting
organization. This season was the culmination of our
change in direction, and I think what Roger Clemens
has done will impact on the Red Sox for many, many
years. Thanks, Danny Doyle."*
—*Haywood Sullivan,
Red Sox CEO*

THE FIRST thing my friends
asked me after I won the Cy Young Award was, "What about the
jinx?" The Cy Young jinx is something real, I guess. Mike Flanagan
won the award in 1979, and hurt his arm. Steve Stone won it in
1980, and won seven games thereafter. Rollie Fingers won it in 1981,
and his elbow blew out the next September. Pete Vuckovich won
it in 1982 and won only six more games in his career. LaMarr Hoyt
won it in 1983 and was 13–18 in 1984. Willie Hernandez was the
one pitcher in the eighties to come back with a good year after
winning it in 1984; but Bret Saberhagen won it in 1985 and fell
to 7–12.

I try to look at this the same way I looked at the so-called Red
Sox jinx that we were facing during the season. I kept saying that
we're a whole new generation of Red Sox players, and that we don't
know, care, or live in the past. When I get asked about the jinx,
I say I'm not everyone else. It's like when Gorman said that I'm
still a physical question mark. He brought up Saberhagen and what

153

had happened to him after he won the Cy Young and got a big contract. I'm not Bret Saberhagen. We're very different people — on and off the field — and I hope I learned something by what happened to him.

I've tried to stay on my off-season program as religiously as possible, because I can see how easy it is to start running around the country, wearing out and not being physically or mentally prepared for the season. Alan Hendricks and I sat down and tried to limit appearances. I agreed to go to a special dinner in Buffalo, the New York Baseball Writers Dinner, and the dinner in Boston. Otherwise, anything I did was supposed to be local — lighting the Christmas tree and getting the keys to the city of Katy, tossing the coin at the Bluebonnet Bowl, things like that. I spoke at some schools about drugs, filmed commercials for Boy Scouts and against smoking, then I went to Waco for Coach Maiorana to talk to high school coaches about conditioning, had my uniform retired at Spring Woods [the only other player ever so honored was 1976 Olympic basketball star Tate Armstrong], and went to the Texas alumni game. Other than that, I've tried to stay on my program.

I lifted and ran almost every day, then began throwing either at the high school or with Capel or (Tigers pitcher) Mark Thurmond after Christmas. People say "you're great, you're great," but I know that they mean that I'm great unless I get off to a 2–5 start in 1987, and I don't want that to happen. I realize that dealing with the expectations that people have placed on my shoulders won't always be easy. If I lose a couple of games, I'm going to be barraged with "what's wrong with Roger Clemens?" stories and I'm going to have my head psychoanalyzed in the papers and I'll hear that I'm getting fat. That comes with the territory. Look at Gooden: he was 17–6, but because he was 24–4 the year before, it was said and written that he had a bad year.

The more success one achieves, the more pressure there is that goes with it, and I accept it. I'd sure rather have the pressure of success than the lack of pressure that goes with anonymity. Also, overcoming the jinx business is great motivation on days when I've gotten back from New York and I want to just sit around the house and relax all day. Some of the things that have been said about my winning the MVP stick with me, too. At the New York banquet in January 1987, Hank Aaron got up and ripped me, saying there was no way that I should have gotten the MVP over Mattingly, and he went on and on about it. The dinner was in New York, so there was a lot of applause and cheering. I was talking to McNamara afterward and Aaron walked up to us and said he hoped that I didn't take it personally and that he didn't mean everything he said. "Some people," I said to Mac, "will do anything for a cheap laugh."

I wish we had Seaver around to talk to about that sort of thing, for he had a way of discussing situations and pressures and setting your head straight. I'll never forget our chat in Texas, or how he helped me and Bruce prepare for pitching in Shea Stadium. I learned a lot in the 1986 season. The play-offs and World Series were learning experiences that I never felt possible, and knowing Seaver should be thrown into the experience bin. Between Seaver, the pennant race, and the postseason, I felt as if I got four years' experience all rolled up in one season, which will only make going on into the next few years easier. I learned a lesson from Seaver that night in Texas that I'll never forget. I learned something from the umpiring incident. I learned a lot about concentration, mental preparation, and letting things bother me in the play-offs and World Series. All of that will help me down the road, just as my injury and rehabilitation experiences were a part of what success I had in 1986.

We'll really miss Seaver (whom the Red Sox haven't re-signed), especially in the clubhouse. The man is so funny and down-to-earth. He was funniest opening his mail. Seaver has one of the most astounding memories of any man on the earth. He remembers names, addresses, handwriting, and he'll never sign cards or pictures twice for the same person because he knows the stuff is being sent to him so they can eventually sell it. He'll look at an envelope, check the address in the left-hand corner, fire it into the trash can, and explain, "I signed three cards for him last year." He'll look at another envelope. "This guy's trying to be tricky, using another name," Seaver would say, "but the handwriting and the postmark don't fool me." One day Hurst was opening his mail and Seaver told him, "I know exactly what that guy's going to ask for." Before Bruce opened it, Tom told him exactly what the letter would say. Hurst opened it, and he was absolutely right.

Another person we'll greatly miss is Lachemann, who has gone to Oakland; he took a lot of heat from the fans but was an extremely important man in our winning. He worked for hours on the charts, ran spring training, threw batting practice, set up defenses . . . sometimes the only word I could use to describe him is awesome.

We all know what Geddy meant to the pitching staff, and when he went to talk contract with Oakland after the '86 season, I was thinking that if he and Lach end up together out there, they will know *everything* about us. Those two talk together and work all the time. Guys like Stapleton, Armas, and Stewart played major roles in winning, also, and while they may have moved on, I'll remember them as part of a pennant-winning team, as I will the guys who left during the season—Mike Brown, Mike Stenhouse, Steve Lyons, Mike Trujillo, and Rey Quinones.

When I look back at the 1986 season, I like to reflect on that afternoon in Winter Haven when Hurst, Can, Nip, and I sat in a circle, held hands and pledged that we'd make it our year. I had my success. Can won sixteen games and by the end of the season was on the road to becoming a twenty-game winner. Hurst was the best pitcher in baseball from August on and, despite his groin pull, was so consistent that only once all season did he allow more than four earned runs; that's amazing. Nip's final numbers weren't what he wanted, but he was great until he got hurt, and his second half was set back by rushing into action for the good of the team beating the Yankees; had we lost that game, maybe the season would have been different. But, more than individual achievements, this was the season that the Red Sox starting pitchers could no longer be called second-class citizens. [Boston starters led the American League in wins with 77, winning percentage at .579, and quality starts with 89. They also led in total decisions, which shows that McNamara left them in to win or lose games. Boyd had the second fewest starts without a decision, 4, of anyone making 30 or more starts. Clemens had 5 in 33, Hurst and Nipper 4 each in 25 and 26, respectively. Clemens, Boyd, Hurst, and Nipper had 97 decisions in 114 starts. There were 14 games at Fenway last season in which three or fewer runs were scored by both teams, combined, a testament to how much they turned it into a pitchers' park.] We had the same competition and comradery that we had at Texas, which is one of the best things in the game. Now that Calvin's had some relieving experience, is starting to do work for his shoulder, and knows people on the ball club, he should be right with us, whether he's a reliever or not.

During the off-season, a controversy arose over the way the players voted to distribute the play-off and World Series shares. It was written that we "stiffed" the clubhouse attendants, ground crew, and players who weren't with us all season and selfishly kept most of the pot for ourselves. It is too bad that the players took such a beating on the subject, for it wasn't intentional. I missed the second meeting because I was pitching, but it was decided that we should give a lot of the money individually. The one area that players didn't want to give money to was for the ground crew, because some players don't get along with Joe Mooney, who runs the crew. When I was a rookie, I went up to Pesky after a night game and asked him if he'd hit me grounders the next day on the mound so I could work on my fielding, something I wanted to do three times a week. "Did you get permission?" asked Pesky. I didn't know what he meant. I never knew you had to have permission to work. The next day we went out there, and as soon as Pesky hit me a ball, Mooney started hollering and threw me off the field. I mumbled something under my breath. He heard it, got mad, and made some comment about my being a rookie. Anyway, I can't work on my fielding at home. It was decided that the hitters should tip the ground crew and that the clubhouse kids, batboys, and other support people should be tipped in addition to whatever grants they got. Rich Zawacki was voted only half a share, but he's done so much for me and for almost everyone that Nip and I bought him a color television.

The 1986 season was more than any twenty-four-year-old should have been able to even dream of. Twenty strikeouts. The fourteen-game streak. The All-Star Game. Winning my twentieth on the anniversary of the operation. The division clincher. The play-offs, especially the fifth game and pitching the pennant clincher. The World Series. The Cy Young. The MVP. It was all thrilling for my entire family, because the one thing that my mother, Randy, and everyone knows is that I'll never forget that I'm a small town kid from Ohio and Texas whose family is—after the Lord—the reason for whatever good has come my way.

The year ended with the arrival of Koby Aaron Clemens, so as 1986 passed, Deb, Koby, and I turned our attention to 1987. The most important reason for me to stay at home and not go out and try to grab every penny I can get off the awards is that I want to spend as much time as possible watching Koby grow. A baseball father has too much time away from his children.

When I was twelve and fantasized about what I wanted, this is what I wanted. So I'm going to enjoy it, never lose sight of my next start, and try to make each one better than the last.

FOR THE RECORD

ROGER'S 1986 STARTS

DATE	OPP	DEC	SCORE	IP	H	R	ER	BB	SO	HR
4/11	@Chi	W	7–2	8.2	6	2	1	5	2	1
4/17	KC	W*	6–2	9	5	2	1	3	7	1
4/22	Det	W*	6–4	6.2	8	3	3	2	10	1
4/29	Sea	W	3–1	9	3	1	1	0	20	1
5/ 4	Oak	W	4–1	8	3	1	1	2	10	1
5/ 9	@Oak	ND	9–6	8.1	8	4	4	0	11	1
5/14	@Cal	W*	8–5	8	6	5	5	5	9	1
5/20	Minn	W	17–7	7	9	5	5	0	4	2
5/25	@Tex	W*	7–1	9	2	1	1	4	8	1
6/ 1	@Minn	W	6–3	8	7	2	2	1	9	1
6/ 6	@Milw	W*	3–0	9	4	0	0	2	8	0
6/11	@Tor	W	3–2	8	4	1	1	2	6	0
6/16	@NY	W*	10–1	9	4	1	1	0	4	0
6/21	Balt	W*	7–2	8	6	2	2	3	6	0
6/27	@Balt	W	5–3	8 +	7	3	2	1	11	2
7/ 2	Tor	L	2–4	7.1	3	4	4	3	8	1
7/ 7	Oak	L	4–6	5 +	7	6	5	0	5	2
7/12	Cal	W*	3–2	9	5	2	1	2	8	0
7/19	@Sea	W*	9–4	8	6	4	4	2	8	1
7/25	@Cal	W*	8–1	9	2	1	1	2	7	0
7/30	@Chi	L*	2–7	4.2	8	3	2	1	1	0
8/ 4	Chi	L	0–1	9	4	1	0	0	6	0
8/10	@Det	ND	9–6	6 +	7	3	3	5	6	1
8/15	Det	W	8–5	7.2	10	5	5	2	6	1
8/20	@Minn	W*	9–1	9	2	1	1	6	6	0
8/25	@Tex	ND*	2–4	8	4	2	2	3	10	1
8/30	Clev	W*	7–3	7	4	3	3	1	11	1
9/ 5	Minn	W	12–2	7	6	1	1	2	4	0
9/10	@Balt	W	9–4	6	6	4	4	4	6	0
9/16	Milw	W*	2–1	9	6	1	1	1	10	0
9/21	@Tor	W*	3–2	8	7	2	2	0	5	0
9/26	Tor	ND*	0–1	9	8	0	0	1	6	0
10/1	Balt	ND*	3–6	1.2	2	1	1	1	0	0

* Following a Red Sox loss

ROGER'S 1986 STATS

W	L	ERA	G	GS	CG	SHO	SV	IP	H	R	ER	HR	HB	BB	SO	WP
24	4	2.48	33	33	10	1	0	254	179	77	70	21	4	67	238	11

THE AL CY YOUNG VOTING, 1986

NAME	TEAM	1ST	2ND	3RD	TOTAL
Roger Clemens	Boston	28	0	0	140
Ted Higuera	Milwaukee	0	11	9	42
Mike Witt	California	0	9	8	35
Dave Righetti	New York	0	5	5	20
Jack Morris	Detroit	0	3	4	13
Mark Eichhorn	Toronto	0	0	2	2

Note: Pitchers receive 5 points for each first-place vote, 3 points for second, and one point for third.

THE 1986 AL MVP VOTING: TOP TEN

NAME	TEAM	1ST-PLACE VOTES	TOTAL POINTS
Roger Clemens	Boston	19	339
Don Mattingly	New York	5	258
Jim Rice	Boston	4	241
George Bell	Toronto		125
Jesse Barfield	Toronto		107
Kirby Puckett	Minnesota		105
Wade Boggs	Boston		87
Wally Joyner	California		74
Joe Carter	Cleveland		72
Dave Righetti	New York		71